PERU TRAVEL GUIDE 2024

A New Pocket Guide with Expert Itineraries, Hidden Gems, and Cultural Insights for Unforgettable Adventures in Machu Picchu, Cusco, Amazon Rainforest, and Beyond

David C. Anaya

Copyright © 2024 by (David C. Anaya)

All rights reserved. No part of this book may be reproduced or transmitted in any form or by any means, electronic or mechanical, including photocopying, recording or by any information storage and retrieval system, without written permission from the author, except for the inclusion of brief quotations embodied in critical reviews and certain other non commercial uses permitted by copyright law.

TABLE OF CONTENTS

INTRODUCTION.................................. 7
Chapter 1: Introduction to Peru............ 11
    A. Overview of Peru................................. 11
    B. Geography of Peru...............................15
    C. History and Culture............................. 19
Chapter 2: Getting to Know Peru........ 24
    A. Language and Communication........... 24
    B. Currency and Banking in Peru............. 30
    C. Transportation.................................35
Chapter 3: Top Destinations in Peru. 40
    A. Lima: The Vibrant Heart of Peru........ 40
    B. Cusco: Gateway to the Inca Empire..... 44
    C. Machu Picchu: The Lost City of the Incas... 48
    D. Arequipa: The White City of Southern Peru... 52
    E. Amazon Rainforest: Exploring Peru's Biodiverse Wonderland............................. 56
    F. Lake Titicaca: Exploring the Sacred Waters of the Andes.................................60

Chapter 4: Exploring Lima..................64
    A. Historic Center.......................................64
    B. Preserving Lima's Heritage....................67
    C. Lima's Culinary Scene: A Feast for the Senses..........76

Chapter 5: Discovering Cusco...............81
    A. Plaza de Armas.....................................81
    B. Sacred Valley..85
    C. Inca Ruins..88
    D. Exploring Cusco's Culinary Scene........92

Chapter 6: Machu Picchu Adventure. 96
    A. Trekking Routes...................................96
    B. Exploring the Inca Trail......................100
    C. Alternative Routes to Machu Picchu 104
    D. Preparation and Tips for Machu Picchu Treks..........108

Chapter 7: Arequipa: The White City..... 113
    A. Santa Catalina Monastery..................113
    B. Colca Canyon.....................................117
    C. City Highlights...................................120
    D. Exploring Arequipa's Surroundings.. 123

Chapter 8: Jungle Experience in the Amazon 128
- A. Wildlife 128
- B. Indigenous Communities 133
- C. Activities 137
- D. Cultural Immersion and Community Visits 140

Chapter 9: Lake Titicaca and Surroundings 147
- A. Floating Islands of Uros 147
- B. Taquile Island 151
- C. Puno City 155
- D. Exploring Lake Titicaca's Mystique ... 159

Chapter 10: Peruvian Cuisine and Dining 163
- A. Traditional Dishes 163
- B. Culinary Experiences 167
- C. Restaurants and Cafes 171
- D. Street Food Delights 175

Chapter 11: Outdoor Adventures in Peru 180
- A. Hiking and Trekking 180

- B. Rafting and Kayaking.......... 184
- C. Paragliding and Biking......... 189
- D. Rock Climbing and Caving...... 193

Chapter 12: Understanding Peruvian Culture.......... 198
- A. Festivals and Celebrations........ 198
- B. Music and Dance............... 202
- C. Arts and Crafts................ 205
- D. Wood Carving................. 208

Chapter 13: Practical Tips for Traveling in Peru.......... 210
- A. Health and Safety............. 210
- B. Packing Essentials............. 215
- C. Etiquette and Customs......... 220
- D. Currency and Money Matters.... 223

Chapter 14: Itineraries for Peru........ 228
- A. 7-Day Highlights Tour......... 228
- B. 14-Day Cultural Immersion..... 232
- C. 21-Day Adventure Expedition... 235

Chapter 15: Farewell and Resources. 239
- A. Travel Resources.............. 239
- B. Further Reading............... 245

CONCLUSION..251

INTRODUCTION

Mr. Samuel, a seasoned traveler with a penchant for cultural exploration, embarked on a journey to Peru filled with anticipation and excitement. Armed with the "Peru Travel Guide 2024," he was ready to immerse himself in the wonders of this South American gem.

His adventure kicked off in Lima, where the bustling streets and historic charm immediately captivated him. Following the guide's recommendations, Mr. Samuel explored the enchanting Miraflores district, savoring the fusion of colonial architecture and modern vibrancy. The guide's insights led him to hidden gems, such as a local café serving the finest Peruvian coffee, providing the perfect start to his Peruvian odyssey.

As he ventured into Cusco, the heart of the Inca Empire, Mr. Samuel marveled at the city's ancient ruins and vibrant markets. The well-crafted itineraries in the guide ensured he didn't miss the breathtaking views of the Sacred Valley and the iconic Plaza de Armas. Guided by the book's expertise, he discovered lesser-known trails leading to Inca ruins, offering a sense of solitude amidst the historical grandeur.

Machu Picchu, a bucket-list destination, awaited Mr. Samuel with the guide unveiling the mysteries of this ancient citadel. He chose the Inca Trail, enchanted by the breathtaking landscapes and guided by the detailed trekking tips provided. Standing atop Machu Picchu, surrounded by mist-covered peaks, Mr. Samuel felt a profound connection to the history and beauty of Peru.

Arequipa, known as the White City, was his next stop. The guide led him through the narrow streets of the Santa Catalina Monastery, a mesmerizing architectural masterpiece. Venturing into the Colca Canyon, he marveled at the breathtaking scenery and engaged with the local communities, thanks to the guide's recommendations on cultural interactions.

Eager for a taste of the Amazon rainforest, Mr. Samuel navigated to the jungle with the guide's assistance. From wildlife encounters to immersive experiences in indigenous communities, every step was enriched by the guide's thoughtful suggestions. Boat rides along the Amazon River and night walks through the lush vegetation added an adventurous flair to his Peruvian escapade.

Lake Titicaca beckoned with its serene beauty and cultural significance. Mr. Samuel explored the floating islands of Uros, gaining insights into the traditional lifestyle of the local people. The guide's chapter on Lake Titicaca provided a perfect blend of history, folklore, and practical travel tips, enhancing his overall experience.

Throughout his journey, the guide became more than just a travel companion; it was a storyteller, a navigator, and a source of inspiration. From sampling local delicacies in Lima to dancing to traditional music in Cusco, Mr. Samuel's days were filled with enriching experiences guided by the carefully curated insights within the pages.

As he concluded his trip, Mr. Samuel reflected on the incredible moments and cultural discoveries. The "Peru Travel Guide 2024" had transformed his adventure into a seamless, immersive exploration. With a heart full of memories, he returned home, not just as a traveler but as someone who had truly lived the magic of Peru.

Chapter 1: Introduction to Peru

Peru, a land of ancient civilizations, breathtaking landscapes, and vibrant cultures, beckons travelers with its rich tapestry of history, geography, and cultural heritage. From the towering peaks of the Andes to the lush Amazon rainforest, Peru offers a diverse array of experiences for adventurers, history enthusiasts, and nature lovers alike.

A. Overview of Peru

Peru, a land of enchantment and wonder, captivates travelers with its rich history, diverse landscapes, and vibrant culture. Situated on the western coast of South America, Peru is a country of immense geographical and cultural diversity, offering visitors a myriad of experiences that range from exploring ancient ruins to trekking through pristine wilderness.

Geographical Diversity:

Peru's geography is characterized by its dramatic contrasts. To the west, the Pacific Ocean kisses its shores, providing stunning beaches and abundant marine life. Inland, the majestic Andes Mountains stretch across the country, boasting some of the highest peaks in the Americas. These mountains not only offer breathtaking vistas but also serve as a playground for outdoor enthusiasts, with opportunities for trekking, mountaineering, and adventure sports.

Beyond the Andes lies the vast expanse of the Amazon rainforest, home to an astonishing array of flora and fauna. The Amazon basin covers more than half of Peru's territory, making it one of the most biodiverse countries on Earth. Exploring the Amazon allows visitors to encounter exotic wildlife, indigenous communities, and pristine ecosystems that have remained largely untouched by human intervention.

In addition to its natural wonders, Peru is also home to diverse ecosystems such as the coastal desert of the Paracas Peninsula, the high-altitude plains of the Altiplano, and the fertile valleys of the Sacred Valley. Each of these regions offers its own unique attractions and opportunities for exploration, from ancient archaeological sites to traditional markets and vibrant cultural festivals.

Cultural Heritage:

Peru's cultural heritage is as rich and diverse as its geography. The country's history is a tapestry woven from the threads of indigenous civilizations, Spanish conquest, African slavery, and immigrant influences from Asia and Europe. The legacy of these diverse cultural influences is evident in Peru's architecture, cuisine, music, and art.

The Inca Empire, which reached its zenith in the 15th and 16th centuries, left behind a legacy of magnificent cities, temples, and fortresses that continue to awe visitors to this day. Machu Picchu, the iconic "Lost City of the Incas," is perhaps the most famous of these archaeological wonders, drawing millions of visitors each year with its mystical aura and breathtaking setting.

Peru's colonial heritage is also evident in its cities and towns, with cobblestone streets, ornate churches, and colonial-era mansions preserving the architectural legacy of Spanish rule. Cities like Lima, Cusco, and Arequipa are living museums, where visitors can stroll through centuries-old plazas, explore hidden courtyards, and immerse themselves in the history and culture of colonial Peru.

Modern Peru:

Today, Peru is a vibrant and dynamic country, where ancient traditions coexist with modern innovations. Its cities are bustling hubs of commerce, culture, and creativity, where skyscrapers rise alongside colonial-era buildings, and traditional markets buzz with activity.

Peruvian cuisine has also gained international acclaim, thanks to its diverse flavors, fresh ingredients, and innovative culinary techniques. From ceviche to causa, anticuchos to alpaca steak, Peruvian cuisine reflects the country's multicultural heritage and its abundant natural bounty.

In conclusion, Peru is a land of endless discovery and adventure, where ancient civilizations, breathtaking landscapes, and vibrant cultures converge to create an unforgettable travel experience. Whether exploring the ruins of Machu Picchu, cruising the waters of Lake Titicaca, or savoring the flavors of Peruvian cuisine, visitors to Peru are sure to be enchanted by its beauty, diversity, and warmth.

B. Geography of Peru

Peru's geography is a marvel of nature, encompassing a diverse range of landscapes and ecosystems that rival the most captivating destinations on Earth. From the rugged peaks of the Andes to the lush expanses of the Amazon rainforest, Peru's geography offers endless opportunities for exploration and adventure.

The Andes Mountains:

Stretching like a spine down the length of the country, the Andes Mountains are one of Peru's most iconic features. With peaks reaching heights of over 6,000 meters (19,685 feet), the Andes are home to some of the world's highest mountains, including Huascarán, Peru's tallest peak. This majestic mountain range not only provides breathtaking scenery but also serves as a natural barrier, dividing Peru into distinct geographic regions.

The Andes are not only a haven for outdoor enthusiasts but also home to vibrant indigenous cultures that have thrived in this challenging environment for thousands of years. Visitors to the Andean highlands can explore traditional villages, witness colorful festivals, and interact with indigenous communities that maintain their ancestral way of life amidst the towering peaks and fertile valleys.

The Amazon Rainforest:

Covering more than half of Peru's territory, the Amazon rainforest is a vast and untamed wilderness teeming with life. Its dense canopy shelters a mind-boggling array of plant and animal species, many of which are found nowhere else on Earth. From elusive jaguars and playful river otters to vibrant macaws and majestic anacondas, the Amazon is a paradise for wildlife enthusiasts and nature lovers.

Exploring the Amazon allows visitors to immerse themselves in one of the world's last great wildernesses, where every step reveals new wonders and surprises. Whether trekking through the jungle, cruising down the winding rivers, or staying in eco-lodges nestled deep in the rainforest, the Amazon offers a truly immersive and unforgettable experience.

Coastal Desert and Pacific Coastline:

To the west of the Andes lies Peru's coastal desert, a stark and arid landscape where sand dunes stretch to the horizon and oases provide welcome respite from the heat. Despite its harsh conditions, the coastal desert is home to thriving cities such as Lima, Peru's capital, where modernity and tradition blend seamlessly against the backdrop of the Pacific Ocean.

The Pacific coastline of Peru is dotted with picturesque beaches, hidden coves, and ancient archaeological sites, offering visitors the chance to relax, surf, and explore the remnants of ancient civilizations that once thrived along the coast. From the mysterious Nazca Lines etched into the desert floor to the colonial charm of seaside towns like Paracas and Máncora, the Peruvian coast is a treasure trove of history, culture, and natural beauty.

In conclusion, Peru's geography is a testament to the wonders of the natural world, with its towering mountains, lush rainforests, and sun-drenched coastlines offering endless opportunities for adventure and exploration. Whether scaling the peaks of the Andes, delving into the depths of the Amazon, or soaking up the sun on the Pacific coast, visitors to Peru are sure to be amazed by the country's breathtaking landscapes and rich biodiversity.

C. History and Culture

Peru's history and culture are deeply intertwined, shaped by millennia of indigenous civilizations, colonial rule, and modern influences. From the ancient Inca Empire to the legacy of Spanish conquest, Peru's rich heritage is reflected in its architecture, art, cuisine, and traditions.

Ancient Civilizations:

Peru is home to some of the oldest civilizations in the Americas, including the Norte Chico civilization, which flourished along the coast more than 5,000 years ago. However, it was the Inca

Empire that left the most enduring mark on Peruvian history. Founded in the 13th century, the Inca Empire reached its peak in the 15th and 16th centuries, encompassing vast stretches of territory and building a network of roads, temples, and fortresses that still stand today.

Machu Picchu, the crown jewel of the Inca Empire, is perhaps the most iconic symbol of Peru's ancient civilizations. This ancient citadel, nestled high in the Andes Mountains, is a testament to the ingenuity and engineering prowess of the Inca people, who constructed it without the use of wheels or iron tools. Today, Machu Picchu attracts millions of visitors each year, drawn by its mystical beauty and awe-inspiring architecture.

Spanish Conquest and Colonial Legacy:

The arrival of Spanish conquistadors in the 16th century marked a turning point in Peruvian history. Led by Francisco Pizarro, the Spanish quickly conquered the Inca Empire and established their own colonial rule. Over the centuries, Peru became the center of Spanish power in South America, with Lima serving as the capital of the Viceroyalty of Peru.

The colonial era left an indelible mark on Peru's culture and society, shaping its architecture, religion, language, and social hierarchy. Colonial cities like Lima, Cusco, and Arequipa are treasure troves of colonial architecture, with ornate churches, grand plazas, and palatial mansions reflecting the wealth and power of the Spanish elite.

Cultural Fusion and Diversity:

Peru's cultural heritage is a vibrant mosaic of indigenous, Spanish, African, and Asian influences. The fusion of these diverse cultures has produced a rich tapestry of traditions, customs, and artistic expressions that are celebrated throughout the country.

One of the most striking examples of this cultural fusion is Peruvian cuisine, which blends indigenous ingredients and cooking techniques with Spanish, African, and Asian flavors. From ceviche and causa to lomo saltado and anticuchos, Peruvian cuisine is a feast for the senses, reflecting the country's diverse culinary heritage and abundance of fresh ingredients.

Modern Peru:

Today, Peru is a modern and dynamic country, where ancient traditions coexist with contemporary lifestyles. Its cities are vibrant hubs of culture, commerce, and creativity, where bustling markets, lively festivals, and avant-garde art scenes thrive alongside skyscrapers and shopping malls.

Despite its modernity, Peru remains deeply connected to its cultural roots, with indigenous communities preserving their traditions and languages, and ancestral rituals and ceremonies still playing a central role in everyday life. From the highlands of the Andes to the depths of the Amazon rainforest, Peru's cultural diversity is a source of pride and identity for its people.

In conclusion, Peru's history and culture are as diverse and captivating as its landscapes, offering visitors a glimpse into the rich tapestry of civilizations that have flourished in this ancient land. Whether exploring ancient ruins, sampling traditional cuisine, or immersing oneself in the vibrant rhythms of Peruvian music and dance, travelers to Peru are sure to be enchanted by its history, culture, and warm hospitality.

Chapter 2: Getting to Know Peru

Welcome to Peru, a land of rich cultural heritage, breathtaking landscapes, and vibrant traditions. In this chapter, we will delve into the essentials of navigating Peru, including language and communication, currency and banking, as well as transportation options.

A. Language and Communication

Peru's linguistic tapestry reflects its rich cultural heritage, shaped by centuries of indigenous traditions, colonial influence, and modern globalization. Understanding the nuances of language and communication is essential for travelers seeking authentic experiences and meaningful connections with the people of Peru.

Spanish: A Cultural Bridge

Spanish stands as the predominant language of Peru, serving as a cultural bridge that unites the country's diverse population. With roots dating back to the Spanish conquest in the 16th century, Spanish permeates all aspects of Peruvian society, from everyday conversations to literature, media, and governance.

For travelers, proficiency in Spanish opens doors to deeper insights into Peruvian culture and facilitates interactions with locals. While many Peruvians in urban areas and tourist destinations speak some level of English, particularly in the hospitality industry, having a basic grasp of Spanish can greatly enhance your travel experience. Even simple phrases like "Hola" (hello), "Gracias" (thank you), and "Por favor" (please) can go a long way in fostering goodwill and building rapport with locals.

Indigenous Languages: Preserving Cultural Heritage

Beyond Spanish, Peru celebrates its indigenous heritage through a multitude of languages spoken by various ethnic groups across the country. Among these, Quechua and Aymara stand out as the most widely spoken indigenous languages, each carrying its own rich history and cultural significance.

Quechua, the language of the ancient Inca Empire, continues to thrive in the Andean highlands and beyond. Its lyrical cadence echoes through bustling marketplaces and tranquil mountain villages, serving as a testament to Peru's enduring indigenous identity. Aymara, spoken primarily in the southern highlands near Lake Titicaca, reflects the resilience of indigenous communities in the face of cultural assimilation and globalization.

Engaging with locals in their native languages offers travelers a window into Peru's diverse cultural landscape and fosters mutual respect and understanding. While learning Quechua or Aymara may prove challenging for most visitors, even a genuine attempt to greet locals in their native tongue can elicit smiles and warm receptions.

Navigating Language Barriers

While language can serve as a bridge, travelers should be prepared to navigate occasional language barriers, especially in remote or rural areas where indigenous languages predominate. In such contexts, non-verbal communication, gestures, and expressions of goodwill transcend linguistic differences and bridge cultural divides.

Fortunately, Peru's tourism infrastructure is well-equipped to accommodate visitors from around the world, with many tourist establishments offering multilingual staff and interpretation services. From guided tours of archaeological sites to culinary adventures in bustling markets, travelers can explore Peru's wonders with confidence, knowing that communication barriers can be overcome with patience and understanding.

In essence, language and communication form the fabric of Peruvian culture, weaving together diverse voices and narratives into a tapestry of shared experiences. Whether conversing with a Quechua-speaking artisan in the Sacred Valley or ordering ceviche in a Lima restaurant, embracing Peru's linguistic diversity enriches the traveler's journey and fosters lasting connections with the people and heritage of this captivating country.

Here are 30 basic Spanish phrases for travelers, along with their meanings in English:

Greetings and Introductions:
1. Hola - Hello
2. Buenos días - Good morning
3. Buenas tardes - Good afternoon
4. Buenas noches - Good evening/night
5. ¿Cómo estás? - How are you?
6. ¿Qué tal? - How's it going?

Polite Expressions:
7. Por favor - Please

8. Gracias - Thank you
9. De nada - You're welcome
10. **Disculpe** - Excuse me
11. **Lo siento** - I'm sorry

Basic Interactions:

12. Sí - Yes
13. No - No
14. ¿Hablas inglés? - Do you speak English?
15. No entiendo - I don't understand
16. ¿Puedes ayudarme? - Can you help me?

Asking for Directions:

17. ¿Dónde está...? - Where is...?
18. ¿Cómo llego a...? - How do I get to...?
19. **A la derecha** - To the right
20. **A la izquierda** - To the left
21. **Recto** - Straight ahead

Ordering Food and Drinks:

22. Quisiera... - I would like...
23. La cuenta, por favor - The check, please

24. ¿Tienen menú en inglés? - Do you have a menu in English?

25. ¿Qué recomiendas? - What do you recommend?

26. Me gusta - I like it

Shopping and Bargaining:

27. ¿Cuánto cuesta? - How much does it cost?

28. Es caro - It's expensive

29. ¿Puedo regatear? - Can I bargain?

30. Está bien - It's okay

These basic Spanish phrases can help travelers navigate various situations and communicate effectively during their travels in Spanish-speaking countries.

B. Currency and Banking in Peru

Navigating Peru's financial landscape is an essential aspect of travel preparation, ensuring smooth transactions and financial security throughout your journey. Understanding the currency system, banking facilities, and exchange options empowers travelers to manage their finances effectively while exploring Peru's diverse attractions.

The Peruvian Sol: Your Currency Guide

The official currency of Peru is the Peruvian Sol (PEN), denoted by the symbol S/. The Sol is subdivided into smaller units called céntimos, with 100 céntimos equaling one Sol. Banknotes come in various denominations, including 10, 20, 50, 100, and 200 Soles, while coins are available in 10, 20, and 50 céntimos, as well as 1, 2, and 5 Soles.

Understanding the value of the Sol relative to your home currency is crucial for budgeting and making informed purchasing decisions while in Peru. Exchange rates may fluctuate, so it's advisable to monitor currency trends and plan your budget accordingly.

Banking Facilities and Services

Peru boasts a robust banking infrastructure, with numerous banks and financial institutions offering a wide range of services to residents and travelers alike. In urban centers and tourist hubs, you'll find an abundance of bank branches, ATMs (Automated Teller Machines), and currency exchange offices, providing convenient access to banking services and cash withdrawals.

ATMs are prevalent throughout Peru, particularly in major cities and tourist destinations. Most ATMs accept major international debit and credit cards, including Visa, Mastercard, and American Express, enabling travelers to withdraw cash in Peruvian Soles or their home currency, depending on the ATM's settings.

Currency Exchange: Tips and Considerations

While currency exchange services are widely available in Peru, it's essential to exercise caution and seek reputable establishments to ensure fair rates and avoid scams. Authorized exchange offices and banks typically offer competitive rates and transparent transactions, making them preferable options for currency exchange.

Before exchanging money, compare rates and fees across different providers to secure the best deal. Be wary of street vendors or unauthorized individuals offering currency exchange services, as they may engage in fraudulent practices or provide unfavorable rates.

Using Credit and Debit Cards

Credit and debit cards are widely accepted in Peru, especially in urban areas, upscale establishments, and tourist-oriented businesses. When using cards for transactions, be mindful of potential foreign transaction fees and currency conversion charges imposed by your bank or card issuer.

To minimize transaction fees and maximize convenience, notify your bank of your travel plans before departing for Peru. This helps prevent potential issues with card authorization and enhances security by alerting your bank to legitimate overseas transactions.

Safety and Security Measures

While Peru is generally safe for travelers, it's advisable to exercise caution when handling cash, using ATMs, or engaging in financial transactions. Keep your cards and cash secure, avoid displaying large sums of money in public, and use ATMs located in well-lit and populated areas.

Consider carrying a mix of cash and cards for flexibility and security. Divide your funds between different pockets or wallets to mitigate the risk of loss or theft. Additionally, keep important financial documents, such as ATM receipts and currency exchange receipts, in a safe and accessible location for reference and record-keeping purposes.

By familiarizing yourself with Peru's currency and banking practices, you can navigate financial transactions with confidence and enjoy a seamless travel experience enriched by the diverse cultural and natural wonders of this enchanting South American destination.

C. Transportation

Exploring Peru's diverse landscapes, ancient ruins, and bustling cities requires efficient and reliable transportation options. From navigating urban centers to embarking on scenic journeys through the Andes, understanding Peru's transportation network is essential for travelers seeking seamless mobility and unforgettable adventures.

Public Transportation: Navigating Urban Centers

Peru's major cities, including Lima, Cusco, and Arequipa, offer extensive public transportation networks comprising buses, micros (minivans), and taxis. In Lima, the capital city, an extensive bus system connects neighborhoods and districts, providing affordable transportation for residents and visitors alike.

Micros, smaller vans often operated by private companies, offer flexible routes and frequent stops, making them a convenient option for short-distance travel within cities. While micros may lack the comfort and amenities of traditional buses, they offer a more localized experience and access to neighborhoods not served by larger buses.

Taxis are readily available in urban areas and can be hailed on the street or through ride-hailing apps like Uber and Cabify. Ensure that taxis are licensed and use meters to avoid overcharging. Negotiate fares in advance for longer journeys or trips to destinations outside the city center.

Inter-city Travel: Connecting Regions and Landmarks

For travelers venturing beyond urban centers, Peru offers an array of transportation options for inter-city travel. Domestic flights provide a convenient and time-saving means of traversing the vast distances between regions, particularly for journeys from Lima to popular tourist destinations like Cusco, Arequipa, and Iquitos.

Long-distance buses, operated by numerous companies, offer an affordable and scenic way to explore Peru's diverse landscapes and cultural heritage. From luxurious sleeper buses equipped with reclining seats and onboard amenities to budget-friendly options with basic comforts, travelers can choose from a variety of bus services tailored to their preferences and budgets.

Train travel also features prominently in Peru's transportation network, with iconic routes like the Andean Explorer connecting Cusco to Lake Titicaca and the Sacred Valley. Train journeys offer a unique perspective on Peru's breathtaking scenery, including towering mountains, verdant valleys, and ancient ruins nestled amidst the Andean foothills.

Regional and Local Transport: Embracing Authentic Experiences

Beyond conventional modes of transportation, Peru's rural and remote areas offer unique travel experiences that capture the essence of the country's cultural and natural diversity. From rustic collectivo vans shuttling passengers between villages to horseback rides through scenic valleys and boat trips along the Amazon River, regional and local transport options immerse travelers in the rhythms of everyday life and the warmth of Peruvian hospitality.

Travelers venturing into the Amazon rainforest can explore remote communities and pristine wilderness areas by boat, experiencing the region's vibrant biodiversity and indigenous cultures firsthand. Whether navigating the Ucayali River or embarking on a multi-day excursion into the Pacaya-Samiria National Reserve, river travel offers unparalleled opportunities for adventure and discovery in one of the world's most biodiverse regions.

In essence, Peru's transportation network reflects the country's rich tapestry of landscapes, cultures, and traditions. Whether traversing bustling city streets or winding mountain roads, each journey unveils new wonders and inspires unforgettable memories, inviting travelers to embark on a transformative exploration of Peru's boundless beauty and allure.

Chapter 3: Top Destinations in Peru

Peru, a land of rich history, stunning landscapes, and vibrant culture, offers travelers a diverse array of destinations to explore. From bustling cities to ancient ruins and natural wonders, Peru captivates visitors with its beauty and charm. In this chapter, we'll delve into some of the top destinations that should not be missed on your journey through this enchanting country.

A. Lima: The Vibrant Heart of Peru

Lima, the capital city of Peru, pulsates with energy, history, and cultural richness. Situated along the Pacific coast, Lima serves as the primary entry point for travelers arriving in Peru, offering a captivating blend of tradition and modernity. From its colonial architecture to its world-renowned gastronomy, Lima entices visitors with its diverse array of attractions and experiences.

Colonial Splendor and Historic Charms

At the heart of Lima lies its historic center, a UNESCO World Heritage Site renowned for its colonial architecture and grand plazas. Plaza Mayor, the main square, serves as the focal point of Lima's historic district, surrounded by architectural marvels such as the Government Palace, the Cathedral of Lima, and the Archbishop's Palace. Stroll along the cobblestone streets lined with colonial mansions adorned with ornate balconies, where you can admire the city's rich architectural heritage.

The San Francisco Convent and its catacombs offer a glimpse into Lima's colonial past, with its impressive Baroque architecture and underground crypts dating back centuries. Explore the labyrinthine passages beneath the convent, where the remains of thousands of individuals are interred, providing insight into Lima's colonial history and religious practices.

Culinary Capital of South America

Lima has earned its reputation as the gastronomic capital of South America, drawing food enthusiasts from around the globe to indulge in its culinary delights. From traditional Peruvian dishes to innovative fusion cuisine, Lima's diverse culinary scene reflects the country's rich cultural heritage and abundant biodiversity.

Ceviche, Peru's national dish, takes center stage in Lima's culinary landscape, featuring fresh seafood marinated in lime juice, chili peppers, and cilantro. Dive into a bowl of creamy causa, a potato-based dish layered with avocado, chicken, or seafood, or savor the smoky flavors of anticuchos, grilled skewers of marinated beef heart served with tangy salsa.

Lima's neighborhoods boast a vibrant street food culture, where food carts and market stalls offer a tantalizing array of snacks and treats. Explore the bustling alleys of Surquillo Market or indulge in authentic Peruvian cuisine at the trendy eateries of

Barranco and Miraflores, where you can savor innovative interpretations of classic dishes paired with Pisco, Peru's national spirit.

Coastal Charms and Modern Marvels

Lima's coastal location offers visitors the opportunity to enjoy its picturesque beaches and scenic waterfront promenades. Take a leisurely stroll along the cliffs of Miraflores, where you can soak in panoramic views of the Pacific Ocean and watch surfers ride the waves below. Paraglide over the cliffs of the Costa Verde or bike along the Malecón, a scenic coastal path that stretches along Lima's coastline.

In contrast to its colonial heritage, Lima boasts modern amenities and infrastructure, with upscale shopping centers, vibrant nightlife districts, and contemporary art galleries dotting the cityscape. Explore the trendy boutiques of Larcomar, catch a performance at the Gran Teatro Nacional, or immerse yourself in Lima's thriving arts scene at the Museo de Arte de Lima (MALI).

From its historic landmarks to its culinary delights and coastal charms, Lima invites travelers to discover the vibrant spirit of Peru's capital city. Whether exploring its colonial heritage, indulging in its culinary delights, or soaking in its coastal beauty, Lima captivates visitors with its unique blend of tradition and modernity.

B. Cusco: Gateway to the Inca Empire

Nestled in the picturesque Andes Mountains, Cusco stands as a testament to Peru's rich Incan heritage and colonial history. Once the capital of the mighty Inca Empire, Cusco enchants visitors with its blend of ancient ruins, Spanish colonial architecture, and vibrant Andean culture. From exploring the cobblestone streets of its historic center to embarking on unforgettable adventures in the Sacred Valley, Cusco beckons travelers to immerse themselves in its timeless beauty and mystical allure.

Inca Ruins and Architectural Marvels

Cusco's historic center, a UNESCO World Heritage Site, serves as the beating heart of the city, where ancient Incan walls mingle with Spanish colonial buildings. Plaza de Armas, the main square, lies at the heart of Cusco's historic district, surrounded by ornate cathedrals, colonial mansions, and bustling markets. Explore the majestic Cathedral of Santo Domingo, built atop the foundations of an Inca temple, and marvel at its stunning blend of Spanish and indigenous architecture.

Venture beyond the city limits to discover the archaeological wonders that lie scattered throughout the Sacred Valley. Explore the ruins of Sacsayhuamán, an ancient fortress overlooking Cusco, where massive stone walls bear witness to the engineering prowess of the Inca civilization. Wander through the terraced slopes of Ollantaytambo and Pisac, where you can marvel at intricately crafted stone temples, agricultural terraces, and ceremonial plazas nestled amidst the Andean mountains.

Cultural Traditions and Andean Mysticism

Cusco's vibrant cultural scene reflects the traditions and customs of its indigenous Quechua population, who continue to preserve their ancestral heritage amidst the modern world. Encounter the vibrant colors and intricate designs of traditional Andean textiles at the bustling markets of San Pedro and San Blas, where skilled artisans showcase their craftsmanship.

Immerse yourself in the mystical rituals and spiritual practices of Andean shamanism, where ancient beliefs and ceremonies endure to this day. Participate in a traditional offering to Pachamama, the Andean earth goddess, or embark on a sacred pilgrimage to the high-altitude sanctuary of Qenko, where you can witness Andean priests performing rituals amidst ancient stone altars and sacred caves.

Gateway to Machu Picchu

As the gateway to the legendary citadel of Machu Picchu, Cusco serves as the starting point for many travelers embarking on the journey of a lifetime. Whether trekking along the famed Inca Trail or opting for the scenic train ride through the Andean highlands, the journey to Machu Picchu is filled with awe-inspiring vistas and unforgettable experiences.

Follow in the footsteps of the ancient Incas as you traverse mountain passes, cloud forests, and high-altitude plateaus on your way to Machu Picchu. Arrive at the Sun Gate at dawn and witness the breathtaking sunrise over the mist-shrouded ruins, where terraced slopes and stone temples blend seamlessly with the natural landscape.

Cusco, with its ancient ruins, cultural traditions, and breathtaking landscapes, offers travelers a glimpse into the heart and soul of Peru's Andean heritage. Whether exploring its historic landmarks, immersing oneself in its vibrant culture, or embarking on a pilgrimage to Machu Picchu,

Cusco captivates the imagination and leaves a lasting impression on all who journey to this mystical city in the clouds.

C. Machu Picchu: The Lost City of the Incas

Perched high in the mist-shrouded peaks of the Andes Mountains, Machu Picchu stands as one of the world's most iconic archaeological sites and a testament to the ingenuity of the Inca civilization. Hidden amidst the lush forests and rugged terrain of southern Peru, this ancient citadel beckons travelers from around the globe to unravel its mysteries and marvel at its breathtaking beauty. From its dramatic mountain setting to its intricate stone architecture, Machu Picchu captivates the imagination and leaves a lasting impression on all who journey to its hallowed grounds.

Mysteries of Machu Picchu

Machu Picchu, meaning "Old Mountain" in the Quechua language, remains shrouded in mystery and intrigue, with its origins and purpose still debated by historians and archaeologists. Believed to have been constructed in the 15th century during the height of the Inca Empire, Machu Picchu served as a royal estate and ceremonial center for Incan rulers, with its remote location and strategic positioning lending it both mystique and significance.

Explore the terraced slopes, stone temples, and intricate agricultural terraces that make up the core of Machu Picchu, where skilled Inca engineers deftly carved and assembled massive stone blocks without the use of mortar. Marvel at the precision and craftsmanship of structures such as the Temple of the Sun, the Intihuatana stone, and the iconic Machu Picchu Observatory, which align with celestial phenomena and reflect the Inca's profound understanding of astronomy and spirituality.

Journey to the Citadel

Accessing Machu Picchu is an adventure in itself, with travelers embarking on a variety of routes and experiences to reach this legendary citadel. The classic Inca Trail trek offers a multi-day hiking adventure through rugged mountain terrain, cloud forests, and ancient Incan ruins, culminating in a dramatic sunrise arrival at the Sun Gate overlooking Machu Picchu.

For those seeking a less strenuous journey, the scenic train ride from Cusco to Aguas Calientes offers panoramic views of the Andean highlands and lush valleys, followed by a bus ride up the winding mountain road to the entrance of Machu Picchu. Whether trekking the Inca Trail or arriving by train, the journey to Machu Picchu is filled with anticipation and excitement, as travelers prepare to behold one of the world's most revered archaeological wonders.

Spiritual and Cultural Significance

Machu Picchu holds profound spiritual and cultural significance for the indigenous Quechua people, who view the citadel as a sacred site imbued with ancestral wisdom and reverence for the natural world. Participate in a traditional offering ceremony led by local Andean shamans, where offerings of coca leaves, flowers, and prayers are made to honor the spirits of the mountains and express gratitude for the blessings of Pachamama, the Andean earth goddess.

As you explore the sacred precincts of Machu Picchu, take a moment to immerse yourself in the spiritual energy and natural beauty that surrounds you, connecting with the ancient wisdom and enduring legacy of the Incas. Whether tracing the footsteps of ancient pilgrims along the Inca Trail or gazing upon the majestic ruins from the heights of Huayna Picchu, Machu Picchu invites travelers to embark on a journey of discovery and wonder, where the past and present converge in a timeless embrace.

D. Arequipa: The White City of Southern Peru

Nestled in the shadow of towering volcanoes and surrounded by dramatic landscapes, Arequipa beckons travelers with its colonial charm, rich history, and stunning natural beauty. Known as the "White City" for its gleaming colonial architecture constructed from white volcanic stone, Arequipa boasts a unique blend of Spanish colonial heritage and indigenous traditions. From exploring its historic center to venturing into the depths of Colca Canyon, Arequipa offers visitors a myriad of experiences that capture the essence of southern Peru.

Colonial Splendor and Architectural Gems

Arequipa's historic center, a UNESCO World Heritage Site, serves as the heart and soul of the city, where colonial mansions, ornate churches, and tranquil plazas transport visitors back in time. Plaza de Armas, the main square, stands as a testament to Arequipa's colonial legacy, surrounded by iconic landmarks such as the Cathedral of Arequipa and the Church of the Society of Jesus, renowned for its intricate Baroque facade.

Wander through the cobblestone streets of San Lazaro and San Francisco, where you can admire the elegant facades and imposing archways of colonial-era mansions, now home to museums, galleries, and artisan workshops. Explore the labyrinthine alleys of the Santa Catalina Monastery, a sprawling convent dating back to the 16th century, where colorful courtyards, winding passages, and tranquil gardens offer a glimpse into the lives of cloistered nuns.

Gateway to Colca Canyon

Arequipa serves as the gateway to Colca Canyon, one of the deepest canyons in the world and a natural wonder that beckons adventurers and nature enthusiasts alike. Embark on a journey into the depths of Colca Canyon, where rugged landscapes, terraced fields, and traditional Andean villages await. Marvel at the majestic flight of the Andean condor as it soars on thermal currents high above the canyon, offering a breathtaking display of nature's splendor.

Discover the traditional villages of Chivay, Yanque, and Coporaque, where indigenous Quechua communities preserve their ancestral traditions and way of life amidst the rugged beauty of the Andean highlands. Immerse yourself in the warmth and hospitality of the local people, who welcome visitors with open arms and share their customs, folklore, and culinary traditions.

Culinary Delights and Gastronomic Traditions

Arequipa's culinary scene reflects the region's rich cultural heritage and diverse culinary traditions, blending indigenous ingredients with Spanish, African, and Asian influences to create a tapestry of flavors and aromas. Indulge in Arequipa's signature dish, rocoto relleno, a spicy pepper stuffed with savory meat and cheese, or savor the hearty flavors of adobo, a traditional stew made with marinated pork and Andean spices.

Explore the bustling markets of San Camilo and Palacio Viejo, where vendors display an abundance of fresh produce, aromatic spices, and artisanal crafts. Sample local delicacies such as chicha morada, a refreshing drink made from purple corn, or indulge in sweet treats like chocotejas, chocolate-covered candies filled with caramel or fruit preserves.

From its colonial heritage to its natural wonders and culinary delights, Arequipa offers travelers a captivating blend of history, culture, and adventure. Whether exploring its historic landmarks, marveling at the beauty of Colca Canyon, or savoring its delicious cuisine, Arequipa invites visitors to experience the magic of the "White City" and discover the wonders of southern Peru.

E. Amazon Rainforest: Exploring Peru's Biodiverse Wonderland

The Amazon Rainforest, a sprawling expanse of lush greenery and vibrant biodiversity, beckons adventurers to explore one of the world's most awe-inspiring ecosystems. In Peru, the Amazon Rainforest covers vast swathes of pristine wilderness, teeming with exotic wildlife, towering trees, and winding waterways. From the depths of the jungle to the tranquil banks of the Amazon River, Peru's Amazon region offers travelers an unforgettable journey into the heart of nature's wonders.

Biodiversity Hotspot

Peru's portion of the Amazon Rainforest is renowned for its incredible biodiversity, boasting a staggering array of plant and animal species found nowhere else on Earth. Venture deep into the jungle, where towering trees form a dense canopy overhead, and exotic creatures roam amidst the undergrowth. Encounter colorful macaws, playful monkeys, elusive jaguars, and majestic anacondas as you navigate the labyrinthine waterways and winding trails of the Amazon.

Explore the rich tapestry of life that thrives within the rainforest, from tiny insects and amphibians to towering hardwood trees and delicate orchids. Embark on guided expeditions led by knowledgeable local guides, who share their expertise and insights into the intricate ecosystems and natural wonders of the Amazon Rainforest.

Immersive Jungle Experiences

Discover the magic of the Amazon firsthand as you embark on a variety of immersive jungle experiences designed to showcase the diversity and beauty of this extraordinary ecosystem. Set out on guided hikes through primary rainforest, where you can observe rare wildlife, learn about medicinal plants, and immerse yourself in the sights and sounds of the jungle.

Navigate winding rivers and tranquil tributaries aboard traditional dugout canoes, where you can explore remote oxbow lakes, spot elusive river dolphins, and witness breathtaking sunsets over the water. Embark on nocturnal expeditions to uncover the secrets of the rainforest after dark, when nocturnal creatures such as owls, frogs, and bats emerge under the cover of darkness.

Cultural Encounters

The Amazon Rainforest is home to numerous indigenous communities, whose ancestral ties to the land stretch back millennia. Engage with indigenous guides and community members who offer unique insights into their traditional way of life, sharing stories, rituals, and customs passed down through generations.

Experience the warmth and hospitality of Amazonian communities as you participate in cultural exchanges, traditional ceremonies, and artisanal workshops. Learn about indigenous traditions such as hunting, fishing, and gathering, as well as the importance of conservation and sustainable resource management in preserving the fragile ecosystems of the Amazon.

Conservation and Sustainability

Peru's Amazon Rainforest faces numerous threats from deforestation, illegal logging, and encroaching development, putting its rich biodiversity and indigenous cultures at risk. Engage in eco-friendly tourism practices that promote conservation and sustainability, supporting local initiatives and community-led conservation efforts that protect the Amazon's precious natural resources.

By choosing responsible tour operators and eco-friendly accommodations, travelers can minimize their environmental impact and contribute to the long-term preservation of the Amazon Rainforest. Take part in reforestation projects, wildlife monitoring programs, and educational initiatives that empower local communities and promote sustainable livelihoods for future generations.

The Amazon Rainforest offers a world of wonders waiting to be discovered, where the rhythm of nature pulses in harmony with the heartbeat of the jungle. Whether exploring its biodiverse landscapes, engaging with indigenous cultures, or supporting conservation efforts, the Amazon Rainforest invites travelers to experience the beauty and wonder of one of the Earth's last great wildernesses.

F. Lake Titicaca: Exploring the Sacred Waters of the Andes

Lake Titicaca, nestled amidst the majestic Andean highlands, stands as a symbol of ancient traditions, cultural heritage, and natural beauty in Peru. Revered by indigenous communities as a sacred and mystical place, Lake Titicaca captivates visitors with its shimmering waters, picturesque islands, and vibrant traditions. From the floating reed islands of the Uros people to the ancient ruins of

Taquile and Amantani, Lake Titicaca offers travelers a glimpse into the rich tapestry of Andean culture and history.

Sacred Waters and Mystical Legends

Lake Titicaca, the largest lake in South America by volume and the highest navigable lake in the world, holds profound significance for the indigenous peoples of the Andes. According to Andean mythology, Lake Titicaca is believed to be the birthplace of the sun god Inti and the Inca civilization, making it a sacred pilgrimage site and a source of spiritual inspiration for generations.

Explore the tranquil shores of Lake Titicaca and marvel at the breathtaking vistas of snow-capped peaks and azure waters that stretch as far as the eye can see. Witness the mesmerizing sunrise and sunset over the lake, where the sky transforms into a canvas of vibrant colors, reflecting the timeless beauty and mystique of this ancient landscape.

Floating Islands of the Uros

Venture into the heart of Lake Titicaca and discover the floating islands of the Uros people, a unique and ancient civilization that has thrived amidst the reed beds of the lake for centuries. Experience the ingenuity and resourcefulness of the Uros people as you explore their intricately constructed islands made entirely of totora reeds, which are continually replenished to maintain their buoyancy and stability.

Engage with local villagers and learn about their traditional way of life, from fishing and weaving to navigating the waters of the lake in traditional reed boats known as "totora" boats. Participate in cultural exchanges and artisan demonstrations, where you can observe the intricate process of weaving and crafting textiles using age-old techniques passed down through generations.

Island Communities and Cultural Immersion

Beyond the floating islands, Lake Titicaca is home to a diverse array of island communities, each with its own unique customs, traditions, and way of life. Journey to the islands of Taquile and Amantani, where indigenous Quechua communities welcome visitors with open arms and offer insight into their rich cultural heritage.

Experience the warmth and hospitality of island communities as you participate in homestay experiences, where you can share meals with local families, participate in traditional ceremonies, and immerse yourself in the rhythms of daily life. Explore ancient archaeological sites, hike to scenic viewpoints

In conclusion, Peru's top destinations invite travelers on a journey of discovery, where ancient mysteries and natural wonders converge to create unforgettable experiences that linger in the heart and soul.

Chapter 4: Exploring Lima

Lima, the vibrant capital of Peru, offers a rich tapestry of history, culture, and gastronomy. From its colonial architecture to its bustling neighborhoods, Lima beckons travelers to explore its diverse landscapes and flavors. In this chapter, we delve into the heart of Lima, uncovering its historic center, the chic district of Miraflores, the bohemian enclave of Barranco, and its renowned culinary scene.

A. Historic Center

The Historic Center of Lima stands as a majestic testament to the city's colonial legacy and architectural grandeur. Stepping into this historic district is akin to entering a time capsule, where the cobblestone streets and ornate facades transport visitors back to Lima's colonial past.

Plaza Mayor: Heart of Colonial Lima

At the heart of the Historic Center lies Plaza Mayor, a sprawling square surrounded by some of Lima's most iconic landmarks. Dominating the plaza is the Government Palace, the official residence of the President of Peru. Its imposing neoclassical facade and changing of the guard ceremony attract visitors from around the world.

Flanking the Government Palace are the Cathedral of Lima and the Archbishop's Palace, both architectural marvels that reflect the city's religious heritage. The Cathedral, with its intricate Baroque facade and ornate chapels, houses the remains of Spanish conquistador Francisco Pizarro. Meanwhile, the Archbishop's Palace showcases elegant balconies and a stunning colonial courtyard, offering a glimpse into Lima's aristocratic past.

Colonial Mansions: Remnants of a Bygone Era

The Historic Center is dotted with colonial mansions that once belonged to Lima's elite families. Among these, Casa Aliaga stands out as one of the oldest residences in the Americas, dating back to the 16th century. This impeccably preserved mansion allows visitors to wander through its elegant rooms adorned with Spanish colonial art and furniture, offering a glimpse into the opulent lifestyle of Lima's early settlers.

Casa de la Riva Aguero is another architectural gem, known for its exquisite Baroque facade and intricately carved wooden balconies. This historic mansion, now a cultural center, hosts art exhibitions, concerts, and lectures, keeping Lima's cultural heritage alive for generations to come.

San Francisco Church and Catacombs: Beneath the Surface

No visit to the Historic Center would be complete without exploring the San Francisco Church and its eerie catacombs. This UNESCO World Heritage Site is renowned for its stunning baroque architecture and lavish interiors, including a magnificent golden altarpiece and intricately painted ceilings.

However, it is the catacombs beneath the church that truly fascinate visitors. A network of underground tunnels and chambers, the catacombs served as Lima's primary burial site during the colonial era. Here, thousands of bodies were interred, their bones arranged in macabre patterns that speak to Lima's complex history of death and devotion.

B. Preserving Lima's Heritage

Despite the passage of time and the challenges of modernization, efforts to preserve Lima's historic center remain steadfast. Restoration projects, cultural initiatives, and heritage conservation programs are underway to safeguard the district's architectural treasures and promote its cultural significance.

Through these endeavors, Lima's Historic Center continues to serve as a living testament to the city's rich history and enduring legacy. As visitors wander its storied streets and explore its timeless landmarks, they become part of a narrative that spans centuries—a narrative of conquest and colonization, of faith and resilience, and of a city that remains forever rooted in its past.

Miraflores: Where Coastal Charm Meets Urban Sophistication

Miraflores, one of Lima's most vibrant districts, captivates visitors with its stunning coastal vistas, lively atmosphere, and modern amenities. Nestled atop cliffs overlooking the Pacific Ocean, Miraflores seamlessly blends natural beauty with cosmopolitan flair, making it a must-visit destination for travelers exploring Lima.

Malecón de Miraflores: A Scenic Stroll by the Sea

The Malecón de Miraflores, a picturesque cliffside promenade, offers breathtaking views of the Pacific coast and serves as the perfect setting for leisurely walks and romantic sunsets. Lined with parks, gardens, and sculptures, the Malecón invites visitors to immerse themselves in the sights and sounds of Lima's coastal landscape.

At Parque del Amor (Love Park), couples can admire the iconic El Beso (The Kiss) sculpture, a testament to love and romance overlooking the sea. This charming park, adorned with mosaic walls and colorful tiles, provides a tranquil escape from the hustle and bustle of city life, inviting visitors to linger and savor the moment.

Parque Kennedy: The Heart of Miraflores

Parque Kennedy, named after the iconic American president, serves as the bustling hub of Miraflores. This vibrant square is surrounded by cafes, restaurants, and shops, making it a popular gathering spot for locals and tourists alike. Street performers and artisans add to the lively atmosphere, entertaining passersby with music, dance, and handmade crafts.

Visitors can relax on park benches shaded by lush trees, observe the resident cats that roam freely, or simply soak in the dynamic energy of Miraflores. Parque Kennedy also hosts cultural events, art exhibitions, and food festivals, reflecting the district's vibrant cultural scene and community spirit.

Larco Museum: Unraveling Peru's Past

For history enthusiasts and art aficionados, the Larco Museum offers a fascinating journey through Peru's pre-Columbian civilizations. Housed in an elegant 18th-century mansion, the museum showcases an extensive collection of ceramics, textiles, and artifacts dating back thousands of years.

Visitors can explore galleries dedicated to ancient Peruvian cultures, including the Moche, Chimu, and Inca civilizations, marveling at intricate pottery, gold jewelry, and ritual objects. The museum's renowned Erotic Gallery, featuring pre-Columbian ceramics depicting scenes of fertility and desire, offers a unique perspective on ancient Peruvian customs and beliefs.

Gastronomic Delights: Dining in Style

Miraflores is also a culinary hotspot, boasting an array of restaurants, cafes, and eateries that cater to every taste and craving. From traditional Peruvian dishes to international cuisine, Miraflores offers a gastronomic adventure for discerning palates.

Travelers can indulge in ceviche, Peru's national dish, at acclaimed seafood restaurants like La Mar or Pescados Capitales. For a taste of Peruvian fusion cuisine, establishments like Maido and Central blend indigenous ingredients with innovative culinary techniques, creating unforgettable dining experiences.

In Miraflores, every meal is an opportunity to savor the flavors of Peru and explore the diverse culinary landscape that defines Lima's gastronomic identity.

Miraflores, with its breathtaking views, vibrant culture, and culinary delights, invites travelers to discover the dynamic spirit of Lima's coastal gem. Whether strolling along the Malecón, exploring ancient artifacts at the Larco Museum, or indulging in exquisite cuisine, Miraflores offers a quintessential Lima experience that captivates the senses and leaves a lasting impression.

Barranco: Bohemian Enclave by the Sea

Barranco, Lima's bohemian neighborhood, exudes a captivating blend of artistic expression, coastal charm, and cultural heritage. Nestled along the cliffs overlooking the Pacific Ocean, Barranco beckons travelers with its colorful streets, eclectic architecture, and vibrant creative scene, making it a haven for artists, musicians, and free spirits.

Colorful Alleys and Street Art

Barranco's streets are adorned with vibrant murals, graffiti, and colorful facades that reflect the neighborhood's creative energy and avant-garde spirit. Wander through the alleys and cobblestone lanes, where every corner reveals a new masterpiece, from whimsical characters to thought-provoking designs.

The artistic expression in Barranco extends beyond the walls, with galleries, art studios, and cultural centers showcasing the works of local and international artists. From contemporary paintings to experimental installations, Barranco's art scene captivates visitors with its diversity and innovation.

Bridge of Sighs: A Romantic Icon

One of Barranco's most iconic landmarks is the Puente de los Suspiros, or Bridge of Sighs, a romantic spot steeped in legend and lore. According to local tradition, couples who cross the bridge and hold their breath while making a wish will have their desires fulfilled.

This charming wooden bridge, adorned with wrought iron railings and overlooking the Pacific, offers stunning views of Barranco's coastline and serves as a picturesque backdrop for romantic encounters and leisurely strolls.

Galleries and Cultural Spaces

Barranco is home to a thriving arts community, with galleries, workshops, and cultural spaces that celebrate creativity and innovation. Explore the eclectic mix of contemporary and traditional art at galleries like Lucia de la Puente and Dedalo Arte, where works by emerging and established artists adorn the walls.

Cultural centers like the MATE Museo Mario Testino showcase photography and visual arts, while the Pedro de Osma Museum offers a glimpse into Peru's colonial past through its impressive collection of paintings, sculptures, and decorative arts.

Bohemian Nightlife

As the sun sets, Barranco comes alive with the pulsating rhythms of its vibrant nightlife scene. From cozy bars and intimate cafes to lively clubs and music venues, Barranco offers something for every nocturnal adventurer.

Experience live music performances at iconic venues like La Noche or Ayahuasca, where local bands and international acts take the stage, captivating audiences with their eclectic sounds and infectious energy. Join the dance floor at clubs like Sargento Pimienta, where salsa, reggae, and electronic beats fill the air, creating an electrifying atmosphere that keeps the party going until dawn.

In Barranco, the night is alive with possibility, offering endless opportunities for exploration, creativity, and connection. Whether immersing oneself in the local art scene, crossing the Bridge of Sighs at sunset, or dancing the night away to the rhythm of the Pacific, Barranco invites travelers to embrace the bohemian spirit and discover the magic of Lima's coastal enclave.

C. Lima's Culinary Scene: A Feast for the Senses

Lima's culinary landscape is a vibrant tapestry of flavors, traditions, and innovations that reflect Peru's rich cultural heritage and diverse culinary influences. From traditional street food to avant-garde gastronomy, Lima's culinary scene tantalizes the taste buds and celebrates the country's bountiful culinary bounty.

Ceviche: Peru's Iconic Dish

At the heart of Lima's culinary identity lies ceviche, a refreshing and flavorful dish that epitomizes Peru's coastal cuisine. Made with fresh fish marinated in citrus juices, onions, and chili peppers, ceviche is a symphony of flavors and textures that delights the palate and showcases Peru's abundant seafood resources.

Locals and visitors alike flock to cevicherias across Lima to savor this beloved dish, with iconic establishments like La Mar, El Mercado, and Canta Rana serving up some of the city's finest ceviche creations. Whether enjoyed with a cold beer or a glass of crisp white wine, ceviche is a culinary experience not to be missed in Lima.

Nikkei Cuisine: Fusion Flavors

Lima's culinary scene owes much to its vibrant immigrant communities, particularly the Japanese immigrants who arrived in Peru in the late 19th and early 20th centuries. Nikkei cuisine, which blends Japanese culinary techniques with Peruvian ingredients and flavors, has become a hallmark of Lima's gastronomic landscape.

Restaurants like Maido, Osaka, and Toshiro's embrace the fusion ethos of Nikkei cuisine, offering innovative dishes that marry the delicate flavors of Japanese sushi and sashimi with the bold spices and vibrant colors of Peruvian cuisine. From tiraditos to sushi rolls infused with aji amarillo and rocoto peppers, Nikkei cuisine is a culinary journey that celebrates the cultural diversity of Peru.

Food Markets: A Gastronomic Adventure

For a taste of authentic Peruvian flavors and local specialties, Lima's food markets offer a sensory feast for the curious traveler. Mercado Surquillo and Mercado San Isidro are bustling hubs of activity where vendors peddle fresh fruits, vegetables, meats, and spices, creating a kaleidoscope of colors and aromas that captivates the senses.

Visitors can sample exotic fruits like lucuma and chirimoya, taste traditional Peruvian snacks like anticuchos and picarones, or savor freshly squeezed juices and smoothies made from tropical fruits. Food stalls and small eateries offer a glimpse into Peru's culinary traditions, with dishes ranging from hearty stews to savory empanadas, providing a true taste of Lima's street food culture.

Gastronomic Tours and Experiences

For those eager to delve deeper into Lima's culinary heritage, gastronomic tours and cooking classes offer immersive experiences that go beyond the plate. Travelers can embark on guided food tours through Lima's neighborhoods, sampling regional specialties, meeting local chefs and artisans, and learning about the cultural significance of Peruvian cuisine.

Cooking classes provide hands-on opportunities to master traditional Peruvian recipes and cooking techniques, from preparing ceviche and causa to crafting Pisco cocktails and desserts. These interactive experiences offer insight into Peru's culinary traditions and foster a deeper appreciation for the flavors and ingredients that define Lima's gastronomic identity.

In Lima, every meal is a celebration of tradition, innovation, and passion—a symphony of flavors that reflects the richness and diversity of Peru's culinary heritage. From the bustling food markets to the fine dining establishments, Lima's culinary scene invites travelers on a culinary journey that delights the senses and leaves a lasting impression.

Chapter 5: Discovering Cusco

Cusco, the heart of the ancient Inca Empire, stands as a testament to Peru's rich cultural heritage and majestic landscapes. As you wander through its cobblestone streets and vibrant markets, you'll discover a city steeped in history and surrounded by breathtaking natural beauty.

A. Plaza de Armas

Nestled at the heart of Cusco, the Plaza de Armas stands as a living testament to the city's rich history and cultural significance. Surrounded by majestic colonial buildings and framed by the towering peaks of the Andes, this historic square serves as the vibrant epicenter of life in Cusco.

History and Architecture

The Plaza de Armas, also known as the "Huacaypata" in the Quechua language, holds a storied past dating back to the time of the Inca Empire. Originally a ceremonial center and marketplace, it was here that the Incas gathered for religious ceremonies, military parades, and cultural celebrations.

With the arrival of the Spanish conquistadors in the 16th century, the plaza underwent a transformation, as colonial architects sought to impose their own vision upon the landscape. Grand cathedrals and palaces were erected, their baroque facades standing in stark contrast to the Inca stonework that lay beneath.

Today, the Plaza de Armas blends seamlessly the architectural styles of two distinct epochs, offering visitors a glimpse into the complex tapestry of Peru's past. From the ornate façade of the Cathedral of Santo Domingo to the elegant arches of the Church of La Compañía de Jesús, each edifice tells a story of conquest, resilience, and cultural fusion.

Cultural Hub

Beyond its architectural splendor, the Plaza de Armas serves as a vibrant hub of activity, where locals and tourists alike converge to soak in the city's vibrant atmosphere. Street vendors peddle traditional handicrafts and colorful textiles, while musicians serenade passersby with the haunting melodies of Andean folk music.

At the heart of the plaza stands the imposing Fountain of the Inca, a symbol of Cusco's indigenous heritage and enduring resilience. Built atop a subterranean aqueduct that dates back to Inca times, the fountain serves as a gathering place for locals and visitors alike, offering respite from the hustle and bustle of city life.

Events and Festivals

Throughout the year, the Plaza de Armas plays host to a myriad of cultural events and festivals that showcase the rich tapestry of Peruvian traditions. From colorful parades during Inti Raymi, the Festival of the Sun, to solemn processions during Holy Week, the plaza pulsates with the energy of a city deeply connected to its past.

One of the most iconic events held in the plaza is the Corpus Christi festival, where elaborately adorned processions wind their way through the cobblestone streets, accompanied by traditional music and dance. For locals, these festivities serve as a poignant reminder of their shared heritage and cultural identity, while for visitors, they offer a window into the soul of Peru.

Overall, in the Plaza de Armas, the past and present collide in a symphony of sights, sounds, and sensations. Here, amidst the grandeur of colonial architecture and the echoes of ancient rituals, travelers can immerse themselves in the rich tapestry of Peruvian culture, forging connections that transcend time and space. As the beating heart of Cusco, the Plaza de Armas invites all who wander its cobblestone streets to become part of its vibrant tapestry, weaving together the threads of history, tradition, and community.

B. Sacred Valley

Stretching along the banks of the Urubamba River, the Sacred Valley unfolds like a verdant tapestry against the backdrop of the towering Andes Mountains. This breathtaking landscape, once the heartland of the Inca Empire, captivates travelers with its picturesque villages, terraced fields, and ancient archaeological sites.

Natural Beauty and Geography

The Sacred Valley owes its striking beauty to its unique geography, which boasts a diverse array of ecosystems and microclimates. Cradled by towering peaks and carved by the meandering Urubamba River, the valley's fertile soils sustain a rich tapestry of flora and fauna, from vibrant orchids to elusive Andean condors.

As visitors journey through the valley, they are treated to a panorama of snow-capped mountains, cascading waterfalls, and emerald-green valleys that seem to stretch into infinity. Whether trekking along ancient Inca trails or exploring hidden gems tucked away in remote corners, the Sacred Valley invites travelers to lose themselves in the splendor of nature's grandeur.

Cultural Treasures

Beyond its natural beauty, the Sacred Valley is also home to a wealth of cultural treasures that bear witness to Peru's rich and storied past. Quaint villages such as Pisac and Ollantaytambo offer a glimpse into traditional Andean life, where Quechua-speaking communities maintain age-old customs and traditions passed down through generations.

One of the most iconic landmarks in the Sacred Valley is the archaeological site of Pisac, where terraced fields cascade down the mountainside like a green staircase to the sky. Here, visitors can wander among ancient temples, ceremonial plazas, and intricately carved rock formations, each bearing silent witness to the ingenuity and architectural prowess of the Inca civilization.

Adventure and Exploration

For adventurous spirits, the Sacred Valley offers a myriad of opportunities to explore its rugged terrain and uncover hidden treasures nestled amidst its mountains and valleys. From adrenaline-pumping whitewater rafting on the Urubamba River to heart-stopping zip line adventures through lush cloud forests, the valley beckons thrill-seekers with its boundless possibilities for exploration and discovery.

One of the most popular attractions in the Sacred Valley is the agricultural terraces of Moray, an ancient Inca site shrouded in mystery and intrigue. Here, visitors can marvel at the precision engineering of circular terraces that served as an agricultural laboratory for the Incas, experimenting with different microclimates and crops to sustain their burgeoning empire.

In the Sacred Valley, nature and culture converge in a symphony of sights, sounds, and sensations that captivate the imagination and stir the soul. Whether tracing the footsteps of ancient civilizations or forging new paths through untamed wilderness, travelers find themselves drawn to the valley's timeless allure, where every mountain holds a story and every valley whispers secrets of the past. As the beating heart of Andean civilization, the Sacred Valley invites all who wander its winding trails and hidden pathways to embark on a journey of discovery, where the boundaries between history and legend blur and the spirit of adventure reigns supreme.

C. Inca Ruins

The remnants of the Inca Empire stand as silent sentinels amidst the rugged terrain of the Andes, beckoning travelers to unravel the mysteries of a bygone era. From the iconic citadel of Machu Picchu to the lesser-known marvels of Sacsayhuamán and Ollantaytambo, the Inca ruins scattered throughout the Cusco region offer a glimpse into the ingenuity and architectural brilliance of one of history's most enigmatic civilizations.

Machu Picchu: Citadel in the Clouds

Perched high atop a mist-shrouded peak, Machu Picchu reigns as one of the world's most iconic archaeological sites, a testament to the engineering prowess and spiritual significance of the Inca civilization. Built in the 15th century and abandoned centuries later, this "Lost City of the Incas" remained hidden from the outside world until its rediscovery by American explorer Hiram Bingham in 1911.

Today, Machu Picchu stands as a UNESCO World Heritage Site and a symbol of Peru's rich cultural heritage, drawing visitors from every corner of the globe to marvel at its terraced fields, ancient temples, and panoramic vistas of the surrounding mountains. As the sun rises over the citadel, illuminating its stone walls with a golden hue, travelers cannot help but feel a sense of awe and wonder at the enduring legacy of a civilization lost to time.

Sacsayhuamán: Fortress of the Sun

Perched high above the city of Cusco, the ancient fortress of Sacsayhuamán stands as a testament to the military prowess and strategic foresight of the Inca Empire. Built from massive limestone blocks weighing up to 300 tons each, the fortress served as a ceremonial center and defensive stronghold, protecting the imperial capital from would-be invaders.

Today, visitors to Sacsayhuamán can marvel at its towering walls and intricate stone carvings, each bearing silent witness to the engineering feats of a civilization that mastered the art of stonemasonry without the use of mortar. As they wander among the ruins, tracing the footsteps of ancient warriors and shamans, travelers cannot help but be transported back in time to a world where gods walked among mortals and empires rose and fell.

Ollantaytambo: Gateway to the Sacred Valley

Nestled at the foot of towering cliffs, the archaeological complex of Ollantaytambo stands as a testament to the ingenuity and strategic vision of the Inca civilization. Built as a royal estate and ceremonial center, the site served as a gateway to the Sacred Valley and a strategic stronghold along the Inca Trail.

Today, visitors to Ollantaytambo can explore its labyrinthine streets and climb its steep terraces, marveling at the precision engineering and architectural splendor of its ancient temples and granaries. As they gaze upon the towering peaks that surround the site, travelers cannot help but feel a sense of reverence for the civilizations that once thrived amidst these rugged mountains, leaving behind a legacy that continues to inspire awe and wonder to this day.

Overall, in the Inca ruins of the Cusco region, the echoes of a bygone era reverberate through the centuries, inviting travelers to embark on a journey of discovery and exploration. Whether tracing the footsteps of ancient civilizations or marveling at the architectural marvels they left behind, visitors find themselves drawn to these sacred sites, where the past comes alive and the spirit of adventure reigns supreme. As the sun sets over the Andes, casting its golden glow upon the ruins below, travelers cannot help but feel a sense of wonder and gratitude for the opportunity to bear witness to the wonders of a civilization lost to time.

D. Exploring Cusco's Culinary Scene

Cusco's culinary scene is a vibrant tapestry of flavors and traditions, reflecting the region's rich cultural heritage and diverse culinary influences. From traditional Andean dishes passed down through generations to innovative fusion cuisine that blends ancient techniques with modern sensibilities, the city's eateries offer a feast for the senses that delights and surprises even the most discerning palates.

Traditional Andean Cuisine

At the heart of Cusco's culinary landscape lies a deep reverence for traditional Andean ingredients and cooking methods. Staples such as quinoa, potatoes, and corn form the backbone of many dishes, celebrated for their nutritional value and cultural significance. From hearty stews like "chupe de camarones" to savory potato dishes like "papa a la huancaína," Andean cuisine embraces simplicity and authenticity, allowing the natural flavors of local ingredients to shine.

Fusion Cuisine

In recent years, Cusco has emerged as a hub of culinary innovation, where chefs draw inspiration from both the past and the present to create dishes that tantalize the taste buds and push the boundaries of traditional gastronomy. Fusion restaurants blend indigenous ingredients with global flavors, resulting in unique culinary creations that celebrate the diversity of Peru's culinary landscape.

Street Food Culture

No visit to Cusco would be complete without exploring its vibrant street food culture, where bustling markets and lively plazas come alive with the aromas of sizzling meats, freshly baked bread, and exotic spices. From savory empanadas and crispy chicharrón to sweet treats like picarones and churros, street vendors offer a dizzying array of delights that cater to every craving and budget.

Pisco and Cocktails

No culinary journey through Cusco would be complete without sampling Peru's national spirit: pisco. This grape-based brandy forms the base of many iconic cocktails, from the classic pisco sour to innovative concoctions that showcase the spirit's versatility and complexity. Whether sipping cocktails in a trendy rooftop bar or sampling artisanal piscos at a local distillery, visitors to Cusco can savor the flavors of Peru's most beloved libation in style.

In Cusco, every meal is a celebration of culture, tradition, and innovation, where the past and present converge in a symphony of flavors and aromas that delight the senses and nourish the soul. From traditional Andean fare to cutting-edge fusion cuisine, the city's culinary scene offers a diverse and dynamic array of options that cater to every taste and preference. Whether dining in a cozy family-run eatery or sampling street food in a bustling market, travelers to Cusco are sure to embark on a gastronomic adventure that leaves a lasting impression and creates memories to savor long after their journey has ended.

In Cusco, every cobblestone tells a story, every plaza echoes with centuries of history. Whether savoring the flavors of Andean cuisine or embarking on a trek through mist-shrouded mountains, the ancient capital of the Inca Empire promises an unforgettable journey through time and culture. Embrace the magic of Cusco, where the past and present converge in a symphony of sights, sounds, and sensations.

Chapter 6: Machu Picchu Adventure

Machu Picchu, nestled high in the Andes Mountains of Peru, stands as a testament to the ingenuity and architectural prowess of the ancient Inca civilization. Visiting this iconic archaeological site offers travelers a profound journey through history, culture, and breathtaking natural landscapes.

A. Trekking Routes

Embarking on a trek to Machu Picchu is a profound journey that offers adventurers the opportunity to immerse themselves in the stunning natural beauty and rich cultural heritage of Peru. The trekking routes to Machu Picchu cater to a diverse range of preferences and fitness levels, each promising a unique and memorable experience.

The Inca Trail

Among the trekking routes to Machu Picchu, the Inca Trail stands out as the most renowned and sought-after option. This ancient pathway traces the footsteps of the Inca civilization, offering hikers a glimpse into the past as they traverse rugged terrain and breathtaking landscapes.

The Inca Trail typically spans approximately 26 miles (42 kilometers) and takes four days to complete, beginning at Kilometer 82 near the town of Ollantaytambo. Along the trail, hikers encounter a series of archaeological sites, including the mesmerizing ruins of Wiñay Wayna and Intipata, before reaching the iconic Sun Gate overlooking Machu Picchu.

Trekking the Inca Trail requires careful planning and preparation, as well as obtaining permits well in advance due to its popularity and conservation efforts. Permits are limited to preserve the integrity of the trail and protect the surrounding environment, making it essential for travelers to secure their spot ahead of time.

The journey along the Inca Trail is not merely a physical challenge but also a spiritual and cultural experience. As hikers ascend through diverse ecosystems, from lush cloud forests to high mountain passes, they gain a deeper appreciation for the ingenuity and resilience of the ancient Incas who constructed this remarkable pathway centuries ago.

Campgrounds along the Inca Trail provide opportunities for rest and reflection amidst the awe-inspiring surroundings. As night falls, the sky comes alive with stars, offering a moment of tranquility and connection with the natural world.

Alternative Routes

In addition to the Inca Trail, several alternative routes offer adventurers the chance to experience Machu Picchu from different perspectives, each with its own unique allure and challenges.

The Salkantay Trek is a popular alternative to the Inca Trail, known for its stunning scenery and diverse landscapes. This challenging trek takes hikers through towering mountain peaks, lush valleys, and pristine glacial lakes, culminating in a breathtaking view of Machu Picchu from the Salkantay Pass.

For those interested in cultural immersion, the Lares Trek offers a glimpse into traditional Andean life. This trek winds through remote villages where travelers can interact with local communities, learn about traditional weaving techniques, and experience the authentic hospitality of the Andean people.

For adventurers seeking a more off-the-beaten-path experience, the Choquequirao Trek presents a rewarding challenge. This lesser-known route leads to the archaeological site of Choquequirao, often referred to as the "sister city" of Machu Picchu. Though demanding, the trek offers a sense of exploration and discovery as hikers uncover the ancient mysteries of this hidden gem.

Whether trekking the Inca Trail or exploring alternative routes, the journey to Machu Picchu is a transformative experience that leaves a lasting impression on the hearts and minds of travelers. Amidst the rugged beauty of the Andes, adventurers forge connections with the past, the land, and the vibrant culture of Peru, creating memories to cherish for a lifetime.

B. Exploring the Inca Trail

The Inca Trail stands as a testament to the ancient engineering marvels of the Inca civilization, offering adventurers a once-in-a-lifetime journey through rugged terrain, lush forests, and breathtaking mountain vistas. Exploring the Inca Trail is not merely a physical endeavor but a spiritual and cultural experience that immerses travelers in the rich tapestry of Andean history and tradition.

Historical Significance

The Inca Trail, known as Qhapaq Ñan in Quechua, served as a vital artery of the Inca Empire, connecting the imperial capital of Cusco with the sacred citadel of Machu Picchu. Constructed over centuries using intricate stone pathways, staircases, and suspension bridges, the trail facilitated trade, communication, and military expeditions across the vast Andean landscape.

For the ancient Incas, traversing the Inca Trail was a sacred pilgrimage, undertaken by priests, nobles, and commoners alike to pay homage to the sacred sites along the way. Today, modern-day trekkers follow in their footsteps, tracing the same path that once echoed with the sounds of Inca warriors and llama caravans.

Trekking Experience

Embarking on the Inca Trail is a multi-day adventure that unfolds amidst breathtaking natural beauty and archaeological wonders. The journey typically begins at Kilometer 82, where trekkers pass through the trailhead and embark on the first leg of their expedition.

As hikers ascend through diverse ecosystems, from verdant cloud forests to high-altitude mountain passes, they encounter a myriad of Inca ruins, including the mesmerizing archaeological site of Llactapata and the intricately terraced agricultural terraces of Phuyupatamarca.

Each day presents its own challenges and rewards, from steep ascents to exhilarating descents, as trekkers navigate through ancient stone staircases and narrow mountain paths. Along the way, experienced guides provide insights into Andean culture, flora, and fauna, enriching the journey with their knowledge and expertise.

Campsites and Hospitality

Campgrounds along the Inca Trail offer respite and camaraderie amidst the rugged wilderness. Each evening, weary trekkers gather around campfires, sharing stories and laughter under the starlit Andean sky.

Meals prepared by skilled cooks offer a taste of Andean cuisine, featuring local specialties such as quinoa soup, grilled alpaca steak, and freshly baked bread. Dining al fresco amidst panoramic mountain views adds to the magic of the Inca Trail experience, creating memories that linger long after the journey has ended.

Arrival at Machu Picchu

The culmination of the Inca Trail journey is the awe-inspiring arrival at Machu Picchu, the crowning jewel of the Inca Empire. As trekkers approach the Sun Gate, known as Inti Punku, they are greeted by the iconic silhouette of Machu Picchu against the backdrop of Huayna Picchu and the surrounding Andean peaks.

The sense of accomplishment and wonder is palpable as travelers explore the ancient citadel, wandering among intricately carved stone temples, terraced gardens, and celestial observatories. Guided tours provide insights into the history and significance of Machu Picchu, unraveling its mysteries and captivating the imagination of all who behold its splendor.

Exploring the Inca Trail is a transformative journey that transcends mere adventure, offering travelers a profound connection to the ancient civilizations and majestic landscapes of the Andes. As footsteps echo through time along this storied pathway, trekkers embark on a voyage of discovery, forging memories and friendships that endure long after the echoes of the trail have faded away.

C. Alternative Routes to Machu Picchu

While the Inca Trail remains the crown jewel of trekking routes to Machu Picchu, alternative pathways offer adventurers unique perspectives and experiences amidst the awe-inspiring landscapes of the Peruvian Andes. From challenging mountain passes to remote Andean villages, these alternative routes promise unforgettable adventures for those seeking to explore Machu Picchu from a different angle.

The Salkantay Trek

The Salkantay Trek is a popular alternative to the Inca Trail, renowned for its stunning scenery and diverse landscapes. This challenging trek takes adventurers on a journey through towering mountain peaks, verdant valleys, and pristine glacial lakes, offering unparalleled views of the majestic Salkantay Mountain along the way.

As trekkers traverse the rugged terrain, they encounter a variety of ecosystems, from lush cloud forests teeming with biodiversity to high-altitude Andean tundra. The highlight of the Salkantay Trek is undoubtedly the crossing of the Salkantay Pass, where travelers are rewarded with panoramic vistas of snow-capped peaks and turquoise lakes stretching to the horizon.

The Lares Trek

For those interested in cultural immersion and off-the-beaten-path exploration, the Lares Trek provides a captivating journey through remote Andean villages and picturesque landscapes. This trek offers a glimpse into traditional Andean life, where travelers can interact with local communities, learn about ancient weaving techniques, and participate in centuries-old agricultural practices.

Along the Lares Trek, hikers are treated to breathtaking views of snow-capped mountains, crystal-clear lakes, and vibrant Andean flora. The route winds through tranquil valleys dotted with terraced fields and grazing llamas, offering a serene escape from the hustle and bustle of modern life.

The Choquequirao Trek

For the intrepid adventurer seeking a truly off-the-beaten-path experience, the Choquequirao Trek presents a challenging yet rewarding journey to the lesser-known archaeological site of

Choquequirao. Often referred to as the "sister city" of Machu Picchu, Choquequirao boasts sprawling terraces, intricate stone structures, and panoramic views of the surrounding mountains.

The Choquequirao Trek takes travelers through remote Andean wilderness, where condors soar overhead and ancient Inca trails crisscross the landscape. The journey to Choquequirao is not for the faint of heart, requiring stamina and determination to navigate steep mountain passes and rugged terrain. However, the sense of discovery and adventure that awaits at the end of the trail makes it a truly unforgettable experience.

Whether hiking the Salkantay, Lares, or Choquequirao routes, alternative pathways to Machu Picchu offer adventurers a chance to explore the diverse landscapes, rich cultures, and ancient mysteries of the Peruvian Andes. As footsteps echo through ancient Inca pathways and pristine wilderness, travelers embark on a transformative journey of exploration and discovery, forging memories and connections that last a lifetime.

D. Preparation and Tips for Machu Picchu Treks

Embarking on a trek to Machu Picchu is an exhilarating adventure that requires careful preparation and planning to ensure a safe and enjoyable journey. From obtaining permits to packing essential gear, adequate preparation is essential for a successful trek through the stunning landscapes of the Peruvian Andes.

Obtaining Permits

For treks along the Inca Trail, securing permits is a crucial first step in the planning process. Permits are limited and often sell out months in advance, especially during the peak season from May to September. Travelers are advised to book their permits well in advance through authorized tour operators to guarantee entry to the trail.

Physical Preparation

Trekking to Machu Picchu involves traversing challenging terrain and high-altitude passes, making physical fitness essential for a comfortable and enjoyable experience. It is recommended to engage in regular cardiovascular exercise, strength training, and hiking practice in the months leading up to the trek to build endurance and stamina.

Packing Essentials

Packing the right gear and essentials is key to staying comfortable and prepared throughout the trek. Essential items to pack include:

- Sturdy hiking boots with ankle support
- Lightweight, moisture-wicking clothing
- Insulating layers for cold nights
- Waterproof jacket and pants
- Sun protection, including sunglasses, sunscreen, and a wide-brimmed hat

- Basic first aid kit with essentials such as bandages, pain relievers, and blister treatment
- Water purification tablets or a portable water filter
- Snacks and energy-boosting foods such as nuts, dried fruits, and granola bars
- Headlamp or flashlight for navigating campsites at night

Acclimatization

Given the high altitude of the Andean region, acclimatization is crucial to prevent altitude sickness and ensure a safe trekking experience. Travelers are advised to spend a few days in Cusco or the Sacred Valley prior to the trek to allow their bodies to adjust to the altitude gradually.

Respect for Nature and Culture

While trekking through the Andean wilderness, it is important to respect the natural environment and cultural heritage of the region. Leave no trace principles should be followed to minimize impact on the environment, including proper waste disposal and avoiding disturbance of wildlife and vegetation.

Similarly, travelers should show respect for local communities and traditions encountered along the trekking routes. Seeking permission before taking photographs and engaging in cultural exchanges with locals fosters mutual respect and understanding.

Overall, preparation is key to a successful and enjoyable trek to Machu Picchu. By obtaining permits in advance, physically preparing for the rigors of the journey, packing essential gear, acclimatizing to high altitude, and showing respect for nature and culture, travelers can embark on a transformative adventure through the majestic landscapes and ancient ruins of the Peruvian Andes. With careful planning and mindful preparation, the journey to Machu Picchu becomes not only an adventure of a lifetime but a profound exploration of history, culture, and natural beauty.

Regardless of the chosen route, trekking to Machu Picchu promises an unforgettable odyssey filled with awe-inspiring landscapes, cultural encounters, and a profound connection to Peru's rich heritage. Prepare for a journey of a lifetime as you embark on this remarkable adventure through the heart of the Andes.

Chapter 7: Arequipa: The White City

Arequipa, known as the White City for its gleaming buildings made of sillar, a volcanic stone, is a captivating destination nestled in the southern region of Peru. With its rich history, stunning landscapes, and cultural gems, Arequipa offers travelers an unforgettable experience.

A. Santa Catalina Monastery

Nestled within the heart of Arequipa lies a hidden gem of unparalleled beauty and intrigue: the Santa Catalina Monastery. This sprawling complex, steeped in history and tradition, offers visitors a rare glimpse into the cloistered world of colonial-era Peru. As you step through its imposing gates, you are transported back in time to an era of devout spirituality and architectural grandeur.

A Legacy of Faith and Tradition

Founded in 1579, the Santa Catalina Monastery was established as a sanctuary for devout women seeking a life of prayer, contemplation, and service to God. Named after Saint Catherine of Siena, the monastery quickly became a beacon of faith in the heart of Arequipa, drawing noblewomen from across the region to its hallowed halls.

For centuries, the monastery remained cloistered from the outside world, its secluded courtyards and labyrinthine passageways serving as a refuge from the tumult of daily life. Within its walls, generations of nuns dedicated their lives to prayer and reflection, creating a sanctuary of unparalleled tranquility amidst the bustling city outside.

Architectural Splendor and Artistic Grandeur

The Santa Catalina Monastery is renowned for its breathtaking architecture and vibrant colors, which reflect the rich cultural heritage of colonial-era Peru. Built from the distinctive white volcanic stone known as sillar, the monastery's intricate facades and ornate courtyards exude a sense of timeless elegance and grace.

As you wander through its labyrinthine corridors, you will encounter a dazzling array of architectural styles, from the ornate Baroque chapels adorned with gilded altars to the tranquil cloisters lined with colorful frescoes and ancient relics. Each corner of the monastery offers a new revelation, a testament to the skill and craftsmanship of the artisans who shaped its storied history.

Exploring the Mysteries Within

Venturing deeper into the heart of the Santa Catalina Monastery, you will discover a world of hidden treasures and sacred spaces waiting to be explored. Pass beneath the iconic arches of the Main Cloister, where sunlight filters through delicate latticework to illuminate the tranquil courtyard below. Marvel at the exquisite beauty of the Chapel of the Virgin of the Immaculate Conception, where centuries-old artworks and religious artifacts speak to the devotion of generations past.

As you meander through the monastery's winding streets and secret gardens, you will encounter echoes of a bygone era, where faith and tradition intertwine to create a tapestry of spiritual beauty. From the humble cells of the nuns to the grandeur of the abbey church, every corner of the Santa Catalina Monastery bears witness to the enduring legacy of Peru's colonial heritage.

In the heart of Arequipa, amidst the bustle of modern life, the Santa Catalina Monastery stands as a timeless testament to faith, tradition, and architectural splendor. As you wander through its storied halls and sacred spaces, you will find yourself transported to a world of grace and tranquility, where the mysteries of the past come alive in vibrant color and exquisite detail. Join us on a journey of discovery as we explore the mystique of this iconic sanctuary and uncover the secrets of colonial-era Peru.

B. Colca Canyon

Stretching across the rugged landscape of southern Peru lies a geological marvel of epic proportions: Colca Canyon. Carved by the forces of nature over millions of years, this breathtaking canyon is not only one of the deepest in the world but also a testament to the awe-inspiring power of Mother Nature. Join us as we embark on a journey to explore the majestic beauty and cultural richness of Colca Canyon.

A Geological Wonder

Colca Canyon's sheer magnitude is enough to leave even the most seasoned travelers spellbound. Plummeting to depths of over 3,270 meters (10,725 feet), the canyon's towering cliffs and rugged terrain offer a dramatic backdrop to the surrounding Andean landscape. Carved by the relentless flow of the Colca River, the canyon's rocky walls reveal a geological tapestry millions of years in the making, where layers of sedimentary rock bear witness to the earth's tumultuous history.

Home to the Andean Condor

One of the most iconic inhabitants of Colca Canyon is the majestic Andean condor, whose graceful flight and impressive wingspan make it a symbol of the Andes Mountains. As the world's largest flying bird, the condor holds a special place in Andean culture and mythology, revered by indigenous peoples as a sacred messenger between the heavens and the earth. Visitors to Colca Canyon have the rare opportunity to witness these magnificent creatures in their natural habitat, as they soar on thermal currents high above the canyon's depths.

Cultural Richness of the Colca Valley

Beyond its breathtaking landscapes, Colca Canyon is also home to a vibrant tapestry of indigenous cultures and traditions. The surrounding Colca

Valley is dotted with traditional villages, where Quechua-speaking communities have preserved their ancestral way of life for generations. Here, ancient agricultural terraces cling to the canyon walls, providing sustenance to local farmers and offering a glimpse into the ingenuity of Andean engineering.

Adventure Awaits

For the intrepid traveler, Colca Canyon offers a myriad of opportunities for exploration and adventure. From hiking along the canyon's rim to soaking in natural hot springs, there is no shortage of ways to immerse yourself in the natural beauty of this awe-inspiring landscape. Trekking routes crisscross the canyon, leading adventurers through remote villages and hidden oases, while guided tours offer insight into the canyon's rich cultural heritage and biodiversity.

Colca Canyon stands as a testament to the raw power and beauty of the natural world, a place where towering cliffs and soaring condors converge to create a landscape of unparalleled splendor. As you explore its rugged terrain and immerse yourself in the cultural richness of the surrounding valley, you will discover a land steeped in history, tradition, and natural wonder. Join us on a journey to Colca Canyon and experience the majesty of Peru's greatest geological treasure.

C. City Highlights

Nestled amidst the majestic peaks of the Andes Mountains, Arequipa beckons travelers with its rich tapestry of history, culture, and culinary delights. From its historic Plaza de Armas to its vibrant markets and iconic landmarks, the city offers a wealth of experiences waiting to be discovered. Join us as we embark on a journey to explore the heart of Arequipa and uncover its most captivating highlights.

Plaza de Armas: A Historic Centerpiece

At the heart of Arequipa lies the Plaza de Armas, a bustling hub of activity and the city's most iconic landmark. Framed by elegant colonial buildings and adorned with lush gardens and ornate fountains, the plaza offers a picturesque setting for leisurely strolls and people-watching. Here, locals and visitors alike gather to admire the beauty of the Cathedral of Arequipa, a magnificent example of Spanish colonial architecture that dominates the plaza's southern edge.

Museo Santuarios Andinos: Unraveling Ancient Mysteries

For those intrigued by the mysteries of the past, the Museo Santuarios Andinos offers a fascinating journey into Arequipa's rich archaeological heritage. Home to the famous Ice Maiden, Juanita, the museum showcases a remarkable collection of Inca artifacts and mummies discovered atop nearby mountain peaks. Visitors can marvel at the well-preserved remains of Juanita, whose sacrifice atop Mount Ampato offers insight into the ancient rituals and beliefs of the Inca civilization.

Culinary Delights: Savoring the Flavors of Arequipa

No visit to Arequipa would be complete without indulging in its rich culinary tradition, which draws inspiration from the diverse landscapes and cultural influences of the region. From hearty soups and savory stews to spicy rocoto relleno and succulent chupe de camarones, the city's gastronomic offerings are as diverse as they are delicious. Visitors can sample local specialties at bustling markets and traditional picanterías, where the flavors of Arequipa come alive in every bite.

Exploring Architectural Gems

Arequipa's architectural landscape is a testament to its colonial past and multicultural heritage, with each building telling a story of the city's rich history and vibrant culture. From the ornate facades of the Santa Catalina Monastery to the elegant arches of the Casa del Moral, architectural gems abound at every turn. Visitors can wander through the city's historic neighborhoods, admiring the intricate details and timeless beauty of its colonial-era buildings.

In the heart of the Andes Mountains, Arequipa beckons travelers with its timeless charm, vibrant culture, and captivating landmarks. From the historic Plaza de Armas to the archaeological treasures of the Museo Santuarios Andinos, the city offers a wealth of experiences waiting to be discovered. Whether savoring the flavors of its culinary delights or exploring its architectural gems, Arequipa invites visitors to experience the heart and soul of Peru in all its splendor. Join us as we embark on a journey to uncover the city's most captivating highlights and immerse ourselves in the magic of Arequipa.

D. Exploring Arequipa's Surroundings

While Arequipa's captivating city center and cultural landmarks offer a wealth of experiences, the surrounding region beckons adventurers with its breathtaking landscapes and hidden treasures waiting to be discovered. Join us as we venture beyond the city limits to explore the natural wonders and cultural gems that await just beyond Arequipa's doorstep.

Majestic Misti Volcano: A Symbol of Arequipa's Majesty

Dominating the skyline with its majestic presence, Misti Volcano stands as a symbol of Arequipa's natural beauty and spiritual significance. Rising to an elevation of over 5,822 meters (19,101 feet), this iconic peak offers a challenging yet rewarding trek for adventurous travelers. As you ascend its slopes, you'll be rewarded with panoramic views of the city below and the surrounding Andean landscape, where snow-capped peaks and sprawling valleys stretch as far as the eye can see.

Andean Highlands: Immersing in Rural Traditions

Venturing into the highlands surrounding Arequipa, travelers are greeted by a landscape of unparalleled beauty and cultural richness. Here, traditional Quechua communities continue to preserve their ancestral way of life, cultivating terraced fields and herding llamas and alpacas amidst the towering peaks of the Andes. Visitors can immerse themselves in rural traditions, participating in age-old rituals and ceremonies that offer insight into the enduring resilience of Andean culture.

Salinas y Aguada Blanca National Reserve: Wildlife and Natural Beauty

Nestled amidst the Andean foothills, the Salinas y Aguada Blanca National Reserve beckons nature enthusiasts with its diverse array of flora and fauna. Home to iconic species such as vicuñas, Andean flamingos, and the elusive Andean fox, the reserve offers a sanctuary for wildlife amidst a backdrop of stunning natural beauty. Visitors can explore its pristine landscapes on guided tours, hiking trails, or scenic drives, marveling at the unique ecosystems that thrive in this rugged terrain.

Sumbay Caves: Ancient Rock Art and Archaeological Wonders

Hidden within the volcanic cliffs of the Andean foothills lies a treasure trove of ancient rock art and archaeological wonders: the Sumbay Caves. Dating back thousands of years, these prehistoric caves are adorned with intricate petroglyphs and paintings that offer a glimpse into the lives and beliefs of ancient Andean civilizations. Visitors can embark on guided tours of the caves, exploring the rich tapestry of images and symbols that adorn their walls and unraveling the mysteries of Peru's pre-Columbian past.

Beyond the bustling streets of Arequipa lies a world of adventure and discovery, where towering volcanoes, pristine reserves, and ancient archaeological sites beckon travelers to explore the wonders of Peru's southern highlands. Whether trekking through the rugged terrain of Misti Volcano, immersing in rural traditions amidst the Andean highlands, or unraveling the mysteries of the Sumbay Caves, the region surrounding

Arequipa offers endless opportunities for exploration and adventure. Join us as we venture beyond the city limits and discover the natural beauty and cultural richness that await in the heart of Peru's southern highlands.

In Arequipa, every corner tells a story, every street beckons exploration, and every moment promises adventure. Whether wandering through ancient monasteries, marveling at natural wonders, or savoring the flavors of Peruvian cuisine, Arequipa invites you to embark on a journey of discovery unlike any other. Join us as we uncover the treasures of the White City and embark on an unforgettable odyssey through the heart of Peru.

Chapter 8: Jungle Experience in the Amazon

The Amazon rainforest in Peru offers an unparalleled adventure for nature enthusiasts and cultural explorers alike. Immersing yourself in the heart of the jungle promises encounters with diverse wildlife, fascinating indigenous communities, and a myriad of activities that showcase the richness of the region's biodiversity and cultural heritage.

A. Wildlife

Venturing into the Amazon rainforest of Peru is akin to stepping into a living, breathing masterpiece of nature—a realm where every rustle of leaves and chorus of birdsong tells a story of resilience and interconnectedness. The sheer diversity of wildlife that inhabits this lush ecosystem is nothing short of awe-inspiring, offering visitors a glimpse into the intricate tapestry of life that thrives amidst the verdant canopy.

A Symphony of Species

At the heart of the Amazon lies a symphony of species, each playing a unique role in maintaining the delicate balance of this extraordinary ecosystem. Among the most iconic inhabitants are the majestic jaguars, apex predators that stalk the forest with silent grace, their golden coats blending seamlessly with the dappled sunlight that filters through the canopy. Though sightings are rare, the mere knowledge of their presence lends an air of mystery and reverence to the jungle.

In the skies above, a kaleidoscope of colors dances against the azure backdrop, as flocks of macaws and parrots paint the heavens with their vibrant plumage. Their raucous calls reverberate through the treetops, signaling their presence to all who inhabit the forest below. Meanwhile, troops of playful monkeys swing effortlessly from branch to branch, their acrobatic antics a testament to the agility and adaptability of life in the canopy.

Beneath the surface of winding rivers and tranquil oxbow lakes, a hidden world awaits discovery. Here, freshwater giants such as the elusive pink river dolphins and prehistoric-looking pirarucu reign supreme, their graceful movements a testament to the age-old rhythms of the Amazon. Giant river otters, with their sleek bodies and inquisitive eyes, navigate the waterways with ease, forging bonds of kinship and cooperation within their close-knit family groups.

Marvels of Microcosms

But the true magic of the Amazon lies not only in its charismatic megafauna, but also in the myriad wonders that inhabit the microcosms of the rainforest. From the iridescent wings of butterflies to the intricate patterns of orchids and bromeliads, every corner teems with life, each organism playing a vital role in the complex web of relationships that sustains the forest.

Venture into the depths of the jungle, and you'll encounter a kaleidoscope of insects, amphibians, and reptiles, each adapted to thrive in their own specialized niche. From the vibrant hues of poison dart frogs to the cryptic camouflage of leaf insects, the diversity of life is staggering, offering endless opportunities for discovery and wonder.

As night falls, a new cast of characters emerges from the shadows, their haunting calls and luminous displays transforming the forest into a realm of mystery and enchantment. Bioluminescent fungi carpet the forest floor, casting an ethereal glow that illuminates the darkness, while nocturnal birds and mammals stir from their daytime slumber to embark on their nightly rituals.

Conservation Challenges

Despite its unparalleled biodiversity, the Amazon faces myriad threats, from deforestation and habitat fragmentation to illegal poaching and climate change. The delicate balance that sustains this remarkable ecosystem hangs in the balance, as human activities continue to encroach upon its pristine wilderness.

Efforts to protect and preserve the Amazon have never been more critical, with initiatives ranging from community-based conservation projects to international collaborations aimed at safeguarding its invaluable resources. By supporting sustainable tourism practices and promoting environmental awareness, travelers can play a crucial role in ensuring the long-term survival of this irreplaceable treasure.

In the Amazon, the line between observer and participant blurs, as visitors become stewards of a fragile ecosystem in need of protection and respect. By embracing the wonder and complexity of the rainforest, we can forge a deeper connection to the natural world and inspire future generations to cherish and preserve the wonders of the Amazon for years to come.

B. Indigenous Communities

Embedded within the vast expanse of the Amazon rainforest are the vibrant and resilient indigenous communities of Peru. For centuries, these communities have thrived in harmony with their natural surroundings, preserving age-old traditions and cultural practices that offer a window into a way of life deeply rooted in the rhythms of the jungle.

Diversity of Cultures

Peru's Amazon basin is home to a rich tapestry of indigenous cultures, each with its own language, customs, and worldview. From the Asháninka of the central highlands to the Shipibo-Conibo of the Ucayali River, these diverse communities embody a profound connection to the land and its resources, viewing themselves not as masters of nature, but as humble stewards entrusted with its care.

Despite centuries of colonization and external pressures, many indigenous groups have managed to preserve their ancestral knowledge and traditions, passing them down through generations in oral histories, songs, and ceremonies. These cultural practices serve not only as a source of identity and pride but also as a testament to the resilience and adaptability of indigenous peoples in the face of adversity.

Traditional Lifestyles

Life in the Amazon is defined by a deep understanding of the natural world and a profound respect for its inhabitants. Indigenous communities rely on traditional hunting, fishing, and gathering techniques to sustain themselves, forging symbiotic relationships with the plants and animals that form the fabric of their existence.

For many indigenous peoples, the forest is not simply a source of sustenance but a sacred space imbued with spiritual significance. Rituals and ceremonies pay homage to the spirits of the land, seeking blessings for bountiful harvests, successful hunts, and harmonious coexistence with the natural world. These sacred practices serve as a reminder of the interconnectedness of all living beings and the importance of honoring the wisdom passed down by ancestors.

Challenges and Resilience

Despite their deep connection to the land, indigenous communities in the Amazon face a host of challenges, including encroachment on their territories, environmental degradation, and loss of cultural heritage. Deforestation, mining, and infrastructure projects threaten not only the physical integrity of ancestral lands but also the spiritual and cultural well-being of indigenous peoples.

Yet, amidst these challenges, indigenous communities continue to demonstrate remarkable resilience and resolve. Through grassroots organizing, advocacy, and cultural revitalization efforts, they are reclaiming their voices and asserting their rights as guardians of the forest. From land titling initiatives to ecotourism ventures that promote sustainable development, indigenous-led initiatives are paving the way for a more equitable and inclusive future in the Amazon.

Cultural Exchange and Community Engagement

For travelers seeking authentic cultural experiences, engaging with indigenous communities offers a unique opportunity to gain insight into centuries-old traditions and ways of life. Homestays, guided tours, and cultural exchanges provide visitors with the chance to immerse themselves in the daily rhythms of village life, learning traditional crafts, participating in rituals, and forging meaningful connections with community members.

It is through these encounters that travelers come to appreciate the profound wisdom and resilience of indigenous peoples, gaining a deeper understanding of the interconnectedness of humanity and the natural world. By fostering mutual respect, cultural exchange, and collaboration, we can build bridges of understanding and solidarity that transcend language and cultural barriers, forging a more inclusive and sustainable future for all who call the Amazon home.

C. Activities

Exploring the Amazon rainforest is not just an adventure; it's a journey of discovery, where every step unveils new wonders and every experience leaves an indelible mark on the soul. From thrilling jungle expeditions to immersive cultural encounters, the Amazon offers a wealth of activities that cater to every adventurer's spirit.

Jungle Treks and Guided Expeditions

Embark on guided jungle treks deep into the heart of the rainforest, where expert guides lead you along winding trails and through dense undergrowth in search of hidden treasures. Traverse towering canopy bridges suspended high above the forest floor, offering breathtaking views of the lush landscape below. As you wander through pristine wilderness, keep your senses attuned to the symphony of nature, from the melodic calls of tropical birds to the rustle of unseen creatures in the underbrush.

For the truly adventurous, multi-day expeditions offer the chance to immerse yourself fully in the rhythms of the jungle, camping under starlit skies and awakening to the chorus of howler monkeys greeting the dawn. As you navigate remote trails and meandering waterways, each day brings new encounters with wildlife and opportunities for exploration, making every moment an adventure to cherish.

Canoeing and River Expeditions

Navigate the labyrinthine waterways of the Amazon by canoe, gliding silently through tranquil rivers and winding tributaries that crisscross the forest. As you paddle gently downstream, keep watch for glimpses of elusive wildlife along the riverbanks, from sunbathing caimans to colorful bird species flitting among the branches.

For those seeking a more immersive experience, multi-day river expeditions offer the chance to explore remote corners of the Amazon inaccessible by land. Traveling by traditional wooden boat, journey deep into the heart of the rainforest, stopping to visit indigenous communities, spot wildlife, and witness the timeless rhythms of river life unfold before your eyes.

Wildlife Watching and Birding

The Amazon is a paradise for wildlife enthusiasts and birdwatchers, boasting an unparalleled diversity of species found nowhere else on Earth. Join expert naturalists and local guides on wildlife watching excursions, where you'll have the chance to spot iconic creatures such as jaguars, giant river otters, and elusive primates in their natural habitat.

For birding enthusiasts, the Amazon offers a veritable feast for the senses, with over 1,500 bird species recorded in the region. From dazzling macaws and toucans to tiny hummingbirds and elusive raptors, the canopy comes alive with a kaleidoscope of colors and melodies, each species adding to the symphony of the rainforest.

D. Cultural Immersion and Community Visits

Immerse yourself in the rich cultural tapestry of the Amazon by visiting indigenous communities nestled along the riverbanks. Engage in cultural exchanges with community members, learning traditional crafts, participating in rituals, and gaining insight into centuries-old traditions passed down through generations.

From traditional dance performances to hands-on workshops in artisanal crafts, community visits offer a glimpse into the daily rhythms of village life, fostering cross-cultural understanding and appreciation. By supporting local initiatives and purchasing handmade crafts directly from artisans, travelers can contribute to the economic empowerment of indigenous communities and the preservation of their cultural heritage.

In the Amazon, adventure awaits at every turn, beckoning travelers to embark on a journey of discovery that transcends the boundaries of time and space. Whether trekking through pristine wilderness, paddling along tranquil waterways, or immersing yourself in the vibrant tapestry of indigenous culture, the Amazon promises an experience like no other—a journey of the soul that leaves an indelible imprint on the heart.

Conservation Efforts

Preserving the biodiversity and cultural heritage of the Amazon rainforest is paramount to ensuring its survival for future generations. Recognizing the ecological significance of this vast wilderness, conservation efforts in Peru's Amazon region are multifaceted, encompassing initiatives aimed at protecting both the natural environment and the indigenous communities that call it home.

Protected Areas and National Parks

Peru boasts a network of protected areas and national parks that safeguard some of the most biodiverse ecosystems on the planet. From the expansive Manu National Park to the remote Pacaya-Samiria National Reserve, these designated conservation areas serve as vital sanctuaries for a vast array of plant and animal species, providing refuge from deforestation, habitat loss, and illegal poaching.

Within these protected areas, strict regulations govern human activities, ensuring minimal disturbance to fragile ecosystems and sensitive wildlife populations. Sustainable tourism practices, such as low-impact trekking routes and responsible wildlife viewing guidelines, help minimize the environmental footprint of visitors while promoting awareness and appreciation for the natural world.

Community-Based Conservation Initiatives

Empowering indigenous communities as stewards of their ancestral lands lies at the heart of many conservation efforts in the Amazon. Through collaborative partnerships and participatory decision-making processes, local communities play a central role in the management and protection of natural resources, drawing upon traditional knowledge and sustainable practices passed down through generations.

Community-based ecotourism initiatives offer travelers the opportunity to engage directly with indigenous communities, providing economic incentives for conservation while fostering cross-cultural exchange and understanding. By supporting locally owned lodges, guided tours, and artisanal cooperatives, visitors contribute directly to the preservation of cultural heritage and the sustainable development of rural economies.

Scientific Research and Monitoring

Scientific research plays a crucial role in understanding the complex dynamics of the Amazon rainforest and informing conservation strategies aimed at its protection. From monitoring biodiversity and tracking wildlife populations to studying ecosystem resilience and climate change impacts, ongoing research initiatives provide valuable insights into the challenges facing the Amazon and the potential solutions needed to address them.

Collaborative research partnerships between government agencies, academic institutions, and nonprofit organizations help bridge gaps in knowledge and promote data-driven decision-making processes. By investing in long-term monitoring programs and interdisciplinary research projects, stakeholders gain a deeper understanding of the interconnectedness of ecological, social, and economic systems within the Amazon, laying the groundwork for informed conservation action.

Advocacy and Policy Reform

Advocacy efforts aimed at raising awareness and mobilizing support for Amazon conservation are integral to driving positive change at local, national, and international levels. From grassroots campaigns to global initiatives, environmental organizations and indigenous rights groups work tirelessly to amplify the voices of those most affected by deforestation, land degradation, and extractive industries.

By advocating for stronger legal protections, land tenure rights, and sustainable development policies, activists and policymakers strive to create an enabling environment for conservation and community empowerment in the Amazon. International agreements such as the Paris Agreement and the Convention on Biological Diversity provide frameworks for cooperation and collective action, highlighting the interconnectedness of global environmental challenges and the urgent need for collaborative solutions.

In the face of mounting threats and unprecedented challenges, conservation efforts in the Amazon are more critical than ever. By embracing principles of sustainability, equity, and respect for indigenous rights, we can work together to safeguard the irreplaceable treasures of the Amazon rainforest for generations to come, ensuring a future where nature thrives and humanity lives in harmony with the natural world.

In the heart of the Amazon, adventure awaits at every turn, beckoning travelers to embark on a journey of discovery, where the rhythms of nature and the spirit of ancient cultures converge in a harmonious symphony of life.

Chapter 9: Lake Titicaca and Surroundings

Lake Titicaca, nestled high in the Andes Mountains between Peru and Bolivia, is the largest lake in South America and one of the highest navigable lakes in the world. Its azure waters, surrounded by breathtaking landscapes and dotted with fascinating islands, hold a rich tapestry of history, culture, and natural wonders waiting to be explored.

A. Floating Islands of Uros

The Floating Islands of Uros stand as a testament to human ingenuity and adaptability, offering a glimpse into a way of life shaped by the tranquil waters of Lake Titicaca. These unique islands, crafted entirely from totora reeds, have been home to the indigenous Uros people for centuries, serving as both a refuge and a source of sustenance in the midst of the vast lake.

Origins and Construction

The history of the Floating Islands dates back to ancient times, when the Uros people sought refuge from conflicts with rival tribes and the expanding Inca Empire. Constructed using layers of totora reeds, which naturally grow in abundance in the shallows of Lake Titicaca, the islands are meticulously woven together to form sturdy foundations that float atop the water's surface.

Sustainable Living

The Uros people have mastered the art of sustainable living, relying on the natural resources of the lake for their survival. The totora reeds not only provide the raw materials for building their homes and islands but also serve as a source of food, medicine, and transportation. The Uros have ingeniously adapted to the challenges of their environment, creating a self-sustaining ecosystem that harmonizes with the rhythms of the lake.

Culture and Traditions

The Floating Islands are not merely a testament to human survival but also a vibrant hub of cultural heritage and traditions. Visitors to the islands have the opportunity to engage with the Uros community, learning about their customs, rituals, and folklore passed down through generations. From traditional music and dance performances to demonstrations of reed weaving techniques, travelers gain insights into the rich tapestry of Uros culture.

Tourism and Sustainability

In recent years, tourism has emerged as a vital economic lifeline for the Uros community, providing opportunities for cultural exchange and economic empowerment. However, the influx of visitors also poses challenges to the delicate balance of life on the islands. Efforts are underway to promote sustainable tourism practices that respect the environment and preserve the cultural integrity of the Uros people.

Preserving a Way of Life

Despite the pressures of modernity, the Uros people remain steadfast in their commitment to preserving their way of life. While technology and modern amenities have found their way onto the islands, the essence of Uros culture endures, rooted in a deep connection to the land and the water that sustains them. As guardians of Lake Titicaca's floating legacy, the Uros people continue to inspire awe and admiration for their resilience and resourcefulness.

The Floating Islands of Uros stand as a living testament to the enduring spirit of the human imagination and the power of community in the face of adversity. As visitors traverse the tranquil waters of Lake Titicaca and set foot upon these remarkable islands, they are invited to embark on a journey through time and culture, where the ancient rhythms of life converge with the boundless wonders of nature. In the heart of South America, amidst the shimmering waters of Lake

Titicaca, the Floating Islands of Uros beckon travelers to discover a world unlike any other, where the past and the present intertwine in a tapestry of resilience and reverence.

B. Taquile Island

Taquile Island emerges from the sapphire waters of Lake Titicaca like a tranquil oasis, offering sanctuary to those seeking respite from the hustle and bustle of modern life. Located on the Peruvian side of the lake, this remote island captivates visitors with its stunning natural beauty, vibrant indigenous culture, and rich tapestry of traditions that have endured for centuries.

Island of Textile Artistry

Taquile Island is renowned worldwide for its exquisite textile artistry, a tradition deeply woven into the fabric of its society. Passed down through generations, the art of weaving holds profound cultural significance, serving as a means of expression, communication, and identity for the island's inhabitants. Taquile textiles are distinguished by their intricate patterns, vibrant colors, and meticulous craftsmanship, each piece reflecting the unique artistic vision of its creator.

Community-Based Tourism

Taquile Island embraces a model of community-based tourism that prioritizes sustainable development and cultural preservation. Unlike many tourist destinations, where external enterprises dominate the landscape, Taquile's tourism initiatives are driven by the island's residents themselves. Visitors are welcomed into the homes of local families, where they can experience firsthand the warmth and hospitality of Taquileño culture. Homestay accommodations offer an authentic glimpse into daily life on the island, fostering meaningful connections between travelers and the communities they visit.

Cultural Immersion and Traditions

A visit to Taquile Island is an immersive journey into the heart of Andean culture, where ancient traditions thrive in harmony with the rhythms of nature. Travelers have the opportunity to participate in traditional ceremonies, learn the art of weaving from master artisans, and savor the flavors of authentic island cuisine. From the rhythmic beats of traditional music to the colorful pageantry of local festivals, Taquile offers a sensory feast for the soul, inviting visitors to embrace the spirit of community and celebration that defines life on the island.

Natural Splendor

Beyond its cultural treasures, Taquile Island captivates visitors with its breathtaking landscapes and panoramic views of Lake Titicaca. Hiking trails crisscross the island, leading adventurers through terraced fields, past ancient ruins, and along rugged cliffs that overlook the azure waters below. As the sun sets over the Andean horizon, painting the sky in hues of gold and crimson, travelers are reminded of the timeless beauty that surrounds them, a testament to the enduring power of nature's grandeur.

Preserving Heritage, Embracing the Future

As Taquile Island welcomes an increasing number of visitors from around the globe, the island's residents remain steadfast in their commitment to preserving their cultural heritage and natural environment. Through sustainable tourism practices, environmental conservation efforts, and community-driven initiatives, Taquileños are charting a course toward a future that honors the traditions of the past while embracing the opportunities of the present.

In the heart of Lake Titicaca, amid the shimmering waters and mist-covered peaks, Taquile Island stands as a beacon of hope and inspiration, where the timeless rhythms of tradition and the boundless spirit of adventure converge in perfect harmony. As travelers venture ashore and explore the wonders of this enchanted island, they are invited to embark on a transformative journey of discovery, where the echoes of the past guide the way forward into a future filled with possibility and promise.

C. Puno City

Puno City, affectionately known as the "Folkloric Capital of Peru," beckons travelers with its vibrant streets, rich cultural heritage, and breathtaking vistas of Lake Titicaca. Situated on the shores of the majestic lake, Puno serves as the gateway to a region steeped in tradition, where the past comes alive in colorful festivals, lively markets, and centuries-old landmarks.

Colonial Charm and Architectural Splendor

Puno's historic center is a captivating blend of colonial charm and Andean grandeur, where ornate churches, cobblestone streets, and elegant plazas evoke a sense of timeless beauty. The Cathedral of Puno, with its imposing facade and intricate Baroque architecture, stands as a testament to the city's religious heritage, while the

Casa del Corregidor offers a glimpse into the colonial administration that once governed the region. As visitors stroll through the city's streets, they are enveloped in the rich tapestry of history that permeates every corner of Puno.

Cultural Crossroads

Puno City serves as a vibrant crossroads of Andean culture, where indigenous traditions blend seamlessly with Spanish influences to create a tapestry of diversity and expression. The city's bustling markets, such as the vibrant Puno Central Market, offer a kaleidoscope of sights, sounds, and aromas, where vendors peddle everything from fresh produce and textiles to handmade crafts and traditional medicines. Travelers are invited to immerse themselves in the vibrant atmosphere of these markets, where the spirit of Andean commerce thrives amidst a backdrop of colorful spectacle.

Gateway to Lake Titicaca

As the gateway to Lake Titicaca and its surrounding attractions, Puno City serves as a launching point for unforgettable adventures on the water. From the bustling harbor, travelers can embark on leisurely boat cruises to explore the islands of Lake Titicaca, including the famed Floating Islands of Uros and the picturesque Taquile Island. Whether navigating the tranquil waters of the lake or hiking along its rugged shores, visitors are treated to unparalleled views of the Andean landscape and the shimmering expanse of the world's highest navigable lake.

Festivals and Celebrations

Puno City pulses with the rhythms of traditional music, dance, and celebration, particularly during its lively festivals and cultural events. The Feast of the Virgen de la Candelaria, held annually in February, is a vibrant spectacle of color and pageantry, featuring elaborate processions, dazzling costumes, and lively music that reverberates through the streets of the city. From the rhythmic beats of the pan flute to the swirling movements of the traditional dance, Puno's festivals offer a feast for the senses and a window into the soul of Andean culture.

Culinary Delights

Puno's culinary scene is a reflection of its diverse cultural heritage, blending indigenous ingredients and flavors with Spanish and international influences. From savory quinoa soups and hearty trout dishes to traditional Andean delicacies such as rocoto relleno and cuy al horno (baked guinea pig), the city's restaurants offer a tantalizing array of culinary delights that showcase the richness and diversity of Peruvian cuisine. Travelers are invited to savor these gastronomic treasures while enjoying panoramic views of Lake Titicaca and the surrounding mountains.

As travelers wander through the colorful streets of Puno City, they are embraced by the warmth and hospitality of its people, whose vibrant culture and indomitable spirit infuse every aspect of life in this enchanting Andean oasis. From its historic landmarks to its lively festivals, Puno invites visitors to discover the heart and soul of Peru's Folkloric Capital, where the past meets the present in a timeless celebration of tradition, heritage, and the enduring beauty of Lake Titicaca.

D. Exploring Lake Titicaca's Mystique

Lake Titicaca, the legendary body of water cradled amidst the Andean peaks, beckons travelers with its mystique and unparalleled beauty. As the largest lake in South America and one of the highest navigable lakes in the world, Lake Titicaca holds within its azure depths a tapestry of natural wonders, ancient legends, and vibrant cultures waiting to be explored.

A Geological Wonder

Nestled at an altitude of over 3,800 meters (12,500 feet) above sea level, Lake Titicaca is a geological marvel that has captivated the imagination of explorers and adventurers for centuries. Formed by tectonic activity millions of years ago, the lake's pristine waters reflect the towering peaks of the Andes, creating a breathtaking panorama that seems to transcend time and space.

Islands of Intrigue

Dotting the surface of Lake Titicaca are a myriad of islands, each with its own unique charm and allure. From the Floating Islands of Uros, crafted from totora reeds by the indigenous Uros people, to the tranquil shores of Taquile Island, where time seems to stand still amidst terraced fields and ancient ruins, these islands offer a glimpse into a world untouched by the passage of time.

Cultural Tapestry

Lake Titicaca is not only a marvel of nature but also a cultural crossroads where indigenous traditions converge with the legacies of ancient civilizations. The shores of the lake are home to indigenous communities whose way of life has remained largely unchanged for centuries, preserving age-old customs, rituals, and languages that speak to the rich tapestry of Andean culture.

Sustainable Tourism

As the popularity of Lake Titicaca as a tourist destination continues to grow, efforts are underway to promote sustainable tourism practices that respect the environment and empower local communities. Community-based tourism initiatives offer travelers the opportunity to engage directly with indigenous cultures, supporting local economies while fostering meaningful cultural exchange and dialogue.

Preserving the Legacy

Lake Titicaca is not merely a destination for travelers but a living legacy that must be cherished and protected for generations to come. Conservation efforts are underway to safeguard the lake's fragile ecosystem and mitigate the impacts of pollution, climate change, and unsustainable development. By raising awareness and fostering a sense of stewardship among visitors and locals alike, we can ensure that Lake Titicaca remains a symbol of natural beauty and cultural heritage for centuries to come.

As travelers embark on their journey across the tranquil waters of Lake Titicaca, they are invited to discover a world of wonder and enchantment, where the ancient rhythms of nature and the timeless traditions of Andean culture converge in perfect harmony. From its mist-shrouded shores to its sun-kissed islands, Lake Titicaca beckons adventurers to explore its mysteries and embrace the magic of this extraordinary destination at the heart of the Andes.

As you journey through Lake Titicaca and its surroundings, each moment unfolds as a captivating exploration of history, culture, and natural beauty, inviting you to discover the heart and soul of Peru's Andean region.

Chapter 10: Peruvian Cuisine and Dining

Peruvian cuisine is a reflection of the country's rich cultural tapestry, blending indigenous ingredients with Spanish, African, Asian, and other immigrant influences. From its traditional dishes to contemporary culinary experiences, Peru offers a vibrant gastronomic landscape that tantalizes the taste buds of visitors from around the world.

A. Traditional Dishes

Peruvian cuisine is a fusion of indigenous ingredients and culinary techniques that have evolved over centuries. From the coastal ceviche to the highland delicacies of the Andes, Peru's traditional dishes reflect the country's diverse geography and cultural heritage.

Ceviche: Peru's Culinary Icon

Ceviche stands as Peru's most iconic dish, celebrated for its vibrant flavors and refreshing qualities. Originating from the coastal regions, ceviche features fresh seafood, typically fish or shellfish, marinated in lime juice and mixed with onions, chili peppers, cilantro, and a hint of garlic. The acidity of the lime juice "cooks" the seafood, resulting in a tender and tangy dish. Ceviche is often served with accompaniments like sweet potatoes, corn, and crunchy cancha (toasted corn kernels), adding texture and depth to the culinary experience.

Lomo Saltado: A Fusion of Cultures

Lomo saltado exemplifies Peru's unique culinary fusion, combining Chinese stir-fry techniques with native Peruvian ingredients. This hearty dish features strips of beef or alpaca, marinated in soy sauce and vinegar, stir-fried with tomatoes, onions, and peppers. The dish is then served atop a mound of steaming rice, accompanied by crispy french fries. Lomo saltado showcases Peru's diverse cultural influences, reflecting the legacy of Chinese immigrants who settled in the country and integrated their culinary traditions with local flavors.

Causa Rellena: Layers of Flavor

Causa rellena is a beloved Peruvian dish that showcases the versatility of potatoes, a staple ingredient in Andean cuisine. The dish consists of layers of mashed yellow potatoes seasoned with lime juice and aji amarillo (yellow chili pepper), filled with a medley of ingredients such as avocado, hard-boiled eggs, and chicken, tuna, or seafood salad. Each layer adds complexity to the dish, creating a harmonious balance of flavors and textures. Causa rellena is often served as an appetizer or light lunch, enjoyed year-round by Peruvians and visitors alike.

Aji de Gallina: Comfort in a Bowl

Aji de gallina is a comforting chicken stew that embodies the warmth and richness of Peruvian home cooking. The dish features shredded chicken bathed in a creamy sauce made from yellow chili peppers, milk-soaked bread, ground walnuts, and a touch of cheese. The sauce is gently simmered until thick and velvety, enveloping the tender chicken in a blanket of flavor. Aji de gallina is traditionally served over boiled potatoes and garnished with olives, hard-boiled eggs, and a sprinkle of fresh herbs, making it a hearty and satisfying meal that resonates with diners of all ages.

Anticuchos: A Taste of Afro-Peruvian Heritage

Anticuchos are skewers of marinated and grilled beef heart, a culinary tradition with roots in Peru's Afro-Peruvian heritage. The dish is marinated in a blend of vinegar, garlic, cumin, and aji panca (dried Peruvian chili pepper), imparting a robust and smoky flavor to the meat. Anticuchos are typically served with boiled potatoes and a tangy salsa made from rocoto peppers, reflecting the spicy and aromatic flavors of Afro-Peruvian cuisine. This street food favorite is enjoyed at festivals, markets, and family gatherings throughout Peru, showcasing the country's diverse culinary tapestry.

In summary, Peruvian traditional dishes offer a culinary journey through the country's history, culture, and diverse landscapes. From the coastal bounty of ceviche to the comforting embrace of aji de gallina, these dishes invite diners to savor the rich flavors and vibrant colors of Peru's gastronomic heritage. Whether enjoyed in a bustling market stall or a fine dining establishment, Peruvian cuisine captivates the senses and leaves a lasting impression on all who indulge in its delights.

B. Culinary Experiences

Exploring Peruvian cuisine goes beyond mere tasting; it's an immersive journey into the heart and soul of the country's culinary traditions. From vibrant market tours to hands-on cooking classes, Peru offers a myriad of culinary experiences that promise to tantalize the taste buds and ignite the senses.

Market Tours: A Feast for the Senses

Embarking on a market tour in Peru is an adventure in itself, a sensory feast that immerses visitors in the vibrant tapestry of local life and flavors. Markets like Lima's Mercado de Surquillo and Cusco's San Pedro Market buzz with energy as vendors hawk their wares, offering an array of colorful fruits, aromatic spices, and exotic ingredients. Engage with local vendors, learn about indigenous produce, and sample traditional snacks like freshly squeezed fruit juices, empanadas, and tamales. From the pungent scent of rocoto peppers to the sweet aroma of lucuma fruit, market tours provide a window into Peru's culinary heritage and the diverse ingredients that shape its cuisine.

Cooking Classes: From Market to Table

For those eager to roll up their sleeves and delve deeper into Peruvian cuisine, cooking classes offer a hands-on opportunity to learn from expert chefs and master the art of traditional dishes. Classes typically begin with a visit to local markets to select fresh ingredients, providing insight into the seasonal produce and culinary customs of the region. Back in the kitchen, participants learn to prepare iconic Peruvian dishes such as ceviche, causa, and lomo saltado, guided by the expertise of seasoned instructors. From mastering knife skills to perfecting the balance of flavors, cooking classes offer a fun and interactive way to deepen one's appreciation for Peruvian gastronomy while creating delicious memories to savor long after the meal is over.

Pisco Tasting: Peru's National Spirit

No culinary journey through Peru would be complete without indulging in a Pisco tasting experience, a celebration of the country's beloved national spirit. Made from distilled grapes, Pisco comes in a variety of styles, from aromatic and floral to bold and fruity. Visitors can explore Pisco distilleries in the picturesque landscapes of the Ica region, where they learn about the production process, from grape cultivation to distillation and aging. Guided tastings allow participants to sample different Pisco varieties, discovering the nuances of each blend and gaining insight into the cultural significance of this iconic Peruvian beverage. Whether enjoyed neat, in a classic Pisco sour, or as part of a creative cocktail, Pisco tasting offers a spirited adventure that captures the essence of Peru's culinary heritage.

Chocolate Workshops: From Bean to Bar

In the lush rainforests of the Amazon and the verdant valleys of the Andes, Peru is home to some of the world's finest cacao beans, the building blocks of delectable chocolate. Chocolate workshops provide a sweet escape into the fascinating world of cacao cultivation and chocolate-making, where participants learn about the history of chocolate, from its ancient origins to its modern-day production. Guided by expert chocolatiers, visitors have the opportunity to roast, grind, and temper cacao beans, crafting their own artisanal chocolate creations infused with Peruvian flavors like Andean salt, lucuma, and Amazonian fruits. Chocolate workshops offer a delicious blend of education and indulgence, inviting participants to awaken their senses and discover the true essence of Peruvian chocolate.

In conclusion, culinary experiences in Peru are as diverse and dynamic as the country itself, offering a tantalizing array of flavors, aromas, and traditions to explore. Whether wandering through bustling markets, mastering the art of Peruvian cooking, sipping Pisco under the Andean sun, or indulging in artisanal chocolate, visitors are invited to embark on a culinary adventure that promises to delight the palate and nourish the soul.

C. Restaurants and Cafes

Peru's culinary landscape is peppered with a diverse array of restaurants and cafes, each offering its own unique interpretation of the country's rich gastronomic heritage. From world-renowned fine dining establishments to cozy neighborhood eateries, Peru's dining scene promises an unforgettable culinary journey for every palate and preference.

Central (Lima): A Gastronomic Expedition

At the helm of Peru's culinary renaissance stands Central, the flagship restaurant of acclaimed chef Virgilio Martínez. Located in the heart of Lima's trendy Miraflores district, Central is renowned for its innovative tasting menus that celebrate Peru's diverse ecosystems and indigenous ingredients. Drawing inspiration from the country's varied altitudes, each dish at Central is a culinary exploration, inviting diners to embark on a sensory journey from the depths of the Amazon rainforest to the soaring peaks of the Andes. With its avant-garde approach to Peruvian cuisine and commitment to sustainability, Central has earned its place among the world's top restaurants, captivating the imaginations of food enthusiasts and culinary connoisseurs alike.

Maido (Lima): A Fusion of Flavors

Maido, led by chef Mitsuharu Tsumura, is a celebration of Peru's vibrant culinary heritage and its fusion with Japanese influences. Located in Lima's stylish Miraflores neighborhood, Maido showcases the art of Nikkei cuisine, a harmonious blend of Peruvian and Japanese flavors and techniques. From delicate tiraditos to innovative sushi rolls, each dish at Maido reflects the restaurant's commitment to quality ingredients, impeccable craftsmanship, and bold flavors. With its sleek, contemporary ambiance and dynamic menu, Maido offers a dining experience that is both elegant and exhilarating, inviting diners to explore the intersection of two rich culinary traditions.

Astrid y Gastón (Lima): Where Tradition Meets Innovation

Astrid y Gastón, founded by renowned chef Gastón Acurio, is a cornerstone of Peru's culinary scene, revered for its creative interpretations of traditional Peruvian dishes. Housed in a stunning colonial mansion in Lima's upscale San Isidro district, Astrid y Gastón offers a refined yet relaxed dining experience that celebrates the country's culinary heritage. From classic ceviche to contemporary takes on Peruvian staples like causa and anticuchos, each dish at Astrid y Gastón is a testament to the restaurant's unwavering commitment to quality, creativity, and innovation. With its warm hospitality, impeccable service, and inspired cuisine, Astrid y Gastón invites diners to embark on a culinary journey that is both nostalgic and forward-thinking.

Café del Museo (Lima): A Culinary Oasis

Nestled within the tranquil grounds of the Larco Museum, Café del Museo offers a serene respite from the hustle and bustle of Lima's city streets. Set amidst lush gardens and ancient pre-Columbian artifacts, the café provides a picturesque backdrop for enjoying classic Peruvian cuisine with a contemporary twist. From hearty causa and flavorful ají de gallina to international favorites like quinoa salad and grilled fish, Café del Museo offers a diverse menu that caters to every taste and appetite. Whether dining al fresco on the sunny terrace or cozying up indoors surrounded by historic artifacts, Café del Museo promises a memorable dining experience that seamlessly blends culture, cuisine, and history.

In summary, Peru's restaurants and cafes offer a tantalizing glimpse into the country's rich culinary heritage, with each establishment telling its own unique story through food, ambiance, and hospitality. Whether savoring innovative tasting menus at Central, exploring the flavors of Nikkei cuisine at Maido, indulging in creative interpretations of traditional dishes at Astrid y Gastón, or dining amidst ancient artifacts at Café del Museo, visitors are invited to embark on a culinary odyssey that celebrates the vibrant flavors and cultural diversity of Peru.

D. Street Food Delights

Peru's street food scene is a vibrant tapestry of flavors, aromas, and culinary traditions that reflect the country's rich cultural heritage and diverse culinary influences. From bustling markets to roadside stalls, Peruvian street food offers a tantalizing array of snacks and treats that cater to every palate and preference.

Anticuchos: The Heart of Peruvian Street Food

Anticuchos are a quintessential Peruvian street food delicacy, beloved by locals and visitors alike for their bold flavors and hearty textures. Originating from Peru's Afro-Peruvian heritage, anticuchos are skewers of marinated and grilled beef heart, seasoned with a blend of vinegar, garlic, cumin, and aji panca (dried Peruvian chili pepper). Served hot off the grill, anticuchos are often accompanied by boiled potatoes and a tangy salsa made from rocoto peppers, offering a spicy and satisfying taste of Peru's culinary heritage.

Picarones: Sweet Temptations

Picarones are a beloved Peruvian dessert that combines the sweetness of pumpkin and sweet potato with the warmth of spices like cinnamon and cloves. The dough is deep-fried to golden perfection, resulting in crispy, yet fluffy, doughnut-like treats that are irresistible to sweet-toothed passersby. Served piping hot and drizzled with a generous dose of chancaca syrup (made from raw cane sugar), picarones are a comforting indulgence that embodies the spirit of Peruvian street food.

Salchipapas: A Satisfying Snack

Salchipapas are a popular street food snack that combines crispy french fries with sliced hot dogs, creating a hearty and satisfying treat that is perfect for on-the-go eating. Served in paper cones and topped with a variety of sauces and condiments, including ketchup, mayonnaise, mustard, and salsa criolla (a tangy onion relish), salchipapas are a favorite among Peruvian families and hungry travelers alike. Whether enjoyed as a quick bite or a late-night indulgence, salchipapas are a comforting reminder of Peru's culinary creativity and ingenuity.

Churros: Sweet and Crispy Delights

Churros are a beloved street food treat that traces its roots to Spain but has been embraced and adapted by Peruvian culture. These deep-fried pastries are made from a simple dough of flour, water, and salt, extruded through a star-shaped nozzle to create their distinctive ridged shape. Crispy on the outside and soft on the inside, churros are dusted with a generous coating of cinnamon sugar and served piping hot, making them a delightful indulgence for those with a sweet tooth. Whether enjoyed on their own or dipped in rich chocolate sauce, churros are a beloved street food staple that brings joy to people of all ages.

In conclusion, Peru's street food delights offer a tantalizing glimpse into the country's culinary soul, with each snack and treat telling its own unique story of tradition, creativity, and cultural heritage. Whether savoring the bold flavors of anticuchos, indulging in the sweet temptation of picarones, enjoying the satisfying crunch of salchipapas, or delighting in the crispy sweetness of churros, visitors to Peru are invited to embark on a culinary adventure that celebrates the vibrant flavors and rich traditions of Peruvian street food.

Peruvian cuisine and dining experiences are integral to understanding the country's culture and history. Whether savoring traditional dishes, embarking on culinary adventures, or dining at world-class restaurants, visitors to Peru are sure to be captivated by its gastronomic treasures.

Chapter 11: Outdoor Adventures in Peru

Peru, with its diverse landscapes ranging from the majestic peaks of the Andes to the lush Amazon rainforest, offers a plethora of outdoor adventures for thrill-seekers and nature enthusiasts alike. Whether you're an avid hiker, an adrenaline junkie, or someone seeking a leisurely bike ride through stunning scenery, Peru has something for everyone.

A. Hiking and Trekking

Peru's diverse landscapes and rich cultural heritage make it a premier destination for hiking and trekking enthusiasts. From ancient Incan trails to remote mountain paths, Peru offers a multitude of hiking and trekking experiences that cater to all levels of adventurers. Whether you seek the iconic views of Machu Picchu or the solitude of high-altitude peaks, Peru's trails beckon with the promise of adventure and discovery.

Inca Trail:

The legendary Inca Trail is perhaps the most renowned trekking route in South America, if not the world. Stretching approximately 26 miles (42 kilometers) through the Andes Mountains, this ancient trail winds its way through cloud forests, high mountain passes, and a stunning array of Incan ruins before culminating at the breathtaking citadel of Machu Picchu.

Trekking the Inca Trail is a once-in-a-lifetime experience that combines awe-inspiring natural beauty with profound cultural significance. Along the way, hikers encounter archaeological sites such as Winay Wayna and Intipata, as well as breathtaking vistas of snow-capped peaks and lush valleys.

The classic Inca Trail trek typically takes four days to complete, with each day presenting its own challenges and rewards. From the grueling ascent to Dead Woman's Pass to the serene beauty of the Sun Gate overlooking Machu Picchu, every step of the journey is imbued with a sense of wonder and adventure.

Due to its popularity, the Inca Trail has limited permits available each day, making advance booking essential. Travelers are also required to trek with a licensed tour operator, ensuring both safety and respect for the environment and cultural sites along the trail.

Cordillera Blanca:

Located in the heart of the Peruvian Andes, the Cordillera Blanca is home to some of the highest peaks in the country, including Huascarán, the tallest mountain in Peru. This pristine mountain range offers a variety of trekking routes, ranging from gentle day hikes to challenging multi-day expeditions.

One of the most popular treks in the Cordillera Blanca is the Santa Cruz Trek, a four-day journey that takes hikers through breathtaking landscapes of turquoise lakes, alpine meadows, and towering glaciers. Highlights of the trek include the stunning views of Mount Alpamayo, considered one of the most beautiful mountains in the world, and the opportunity to interact with local Quechua communities along the way.

For more experienced trekkers, the Huayhuash Circuit offers a challenging adventure through remote valleys and high mountain passes, showcasing the rugged beauty of the Andes in all its glory. This demanding trek typically takes around 10 days to complete and rewards hikers with unparalleled views of snow-capped peaks and pristine wilderness.

Colca Canyon:

Twice as deep as the Grand Canyon, Colca Canyon is one of the deepest canyons in the world and a popular destination for adventurous trekkers. Located in the Arequipa region of southern Peru, Colca Canyon offers a range of trekking options, from day hikes along the canyon rim to multi-day expeditions descending into the depths of the canyon itself.

The most famous trek in Colca Canyon is the Colca Trek, a two- or three-day journey that takes hikers from the picturesque village of Cabanaconde down into the canyon and back again. Along the way, trekkers are treated to spectacular views of terraced fields, towering cliffs, and the dramatic flight of the Andean condor, one of the largest birds in the world.

Whether you're drawn to the ancient mysteries of the Inca Trail, the rugged beauty of the Cordillera Blanca, or the awe-inspiring depths of Colca Canyon, Peru's hiking and trekking opportunities promise an unforgettable adventure amidst some of the most breathtaking landscapes on Earth.

B. Rafting and Kayaking

Peru's diverse network of rivers offers unparalleled opportunities for whitewater rafting and kayaking adventures. From exhilarating rapids to tranquil stretches of water, Peru's rivers cater to paddlers of all skill levels, providing thrills, challenges, and unforgettable experiences amidst some of the most stunning landscapes on the planet.

Apurimac River:

Known as one of the best whitewater rafting destinations in the world, the Apurimac River flows through the heart of the Peruvian Andes, carving its way through deep canyons and remote wilderness. The river's name, which means "speaking God" in the Quechua language, hints at its sacred significance to the local indigenous communities.

Rafting the Apurimac River offers adrenaline-pumping excitement as paddlers navigate challenging Class III to V rapids, including infamous stretches like "Toothache" and "You First." Along the way, rafters are treated to breathtaking scenery, including towering cliffs, lush jungle vegetation, and glimpses of Andean wildlife such as Andean condors and torrent ducks.

Multi-day rafting expeditions on the Apurimac River typically include camping under the stars on sandy riverbanks, enjoying hearty meals cooked over an open fire, and soaking in natural hot springs along the way. Experienced guides ensure safety and provide insight into the cultural and natural history of the region, making the Apurimac River rafting experience both thrilling and enriching.

Urubamba River:

Flowing through the Sacred Valley of the Incas, the Urubamba River offers a variety of rafting experiences suitable for adventurers of all levels. From gentle Class II rapids perfect for families to adrenaline-charged Class IV sections that challenge even the most experienced paddlers, the Urubamba River has something for everyone.

One of the most popular rafting sections on the Urubamba River is the route from Ollantaytambo to Chilca, which offers a thrilling combination of exciting rapids and stunning scenery. Paddlers navigate through narrow canyons, past ancient Incan terraces, and alongside picturesque Andean villages, creating memories that will last a lifetime.

For those seeking a more leisurely experience, the lower sections of the Urubamba River provide opportunities for scenic float trips, where rafters can relax and soak in the beauty of the Sacred Valley at a more relaxed pace. Whether you're seeking adrenaline-fueled adventure or tranquil relaxation, the Urubamba River delivers an unforgettable rafting experience amidst the breathtaking landscapes of Peru.

Tambopata River:

Deep in the heart of the Amazon rainforest, the Tambopata River offers a unique kayaking experience amidst some of the most biodiverse ecosystems on Earth. Paddlers glide silently through pristine rainforest, exploring narrow channels and oxbow lakes teeming with wildlife.

Kayaking on the Tambopata River provides the opportunity to encounter a dazzling array of wildlife, including colorful birds such as macaws and toucans, playful river otters, and elusive jaguars. Guided kayaking expeditions also offer the chance to learn about the intricate relationships between the plants, animals, and indigenous communities that call the Amazon home.

In addition to wildlife encounters, kayakers on the Tambopata River can immerse themselves in the sights and sounds of the rainforest, from the haunting calls of howler monkeys to the vibrant colors of tropical flowers and butterflies. With each paddle stroke, kayakers embark on a journey of exploration and discovery, uncovering the hidden wonders of the Amazon rainforest in Peru.

C. Paragliding and Biking

Peru's diverse landscapes, from coastal cliffs to mountainous terrain, offer thrilling opportunities for paragliding and biking enthusiasts. Whether you're soaring high above the Pacific coastline or pedaling through ancient Incan ruins, Peru's outdoor adventures promise unforgettable experiences for adrenaline junkies and nature lovers alike.

Paragliding in Lima:

Lima's coastal cliffs provide the perfect launchpad for exhilarating paragliding adventures high above the Pacific Ocean. With its consistent sea breezes and stunning panoramic views, Lima offers one of the best paragliding experiences in South America.

From the cliffs of Miraflores and Barranco, paragliders take to the skies, soaring like birds as they enjoy breathtaking vistas of Lima's modern skyline, sandy beaches, and crashing waves below. Experienced tandem pilots ensure a safe and thrilling ride, allowing adventurers to experience the sensation of free flight with unmatched views of the Peruvian coast.

Paragliding in Lima is a truly unforgettable experience, combining the adrenaline rush of flight with the natural beauty of Peru's rugged coastline.

Mountain Biking in the Sacred Valley:

The Sacred Valley of the Incas, with its stunning landscapes and rich cultural heritage, offers endless opportunities for mountain biking adventures. From high-altitude passes to ancient Incan trails, the Sacred Valley provides a diverse array of terrain for bikers of all skill levels.

One of the most popular mountain biking routes in the Sacred Valley is the descent from the high-altitude village of Chinchero to the archaeological site of Moray and the salt pans of Maras. This exhilarating downhill ride takes bikers through breathtaking scenery, including terraced fields, Andean villages, and panoramic views of snow-capped peaks.

For more experienced riders, the challenging trails around Ollantaytambo and Pisac offer technical descents and adrenaline-pumping singletrack through rugged terrain. Guided mountain biking tours provide the opportunity to explore hidden corners of the Sacred Valley, encounter local Quechua communities, and learn about the ancient Incan civilization that once thrived in this spectacular landscape.

Mountain biking in the Sacred Valley is a thrilling way to experience the beauty and history of Peru's Andean region, offering adventurers an immersive journey through some of the most stunning landscapes in the world.

Nazca Lines Overflight:

For a truly unique adventure in Peru, take to the skies in a small aircraft for an unforgettable overflight of the enigmatic Nazca Lines. Located in the arid desert plains of southern Peru, the Nazca Lines are a series of ancient geoglyphs etched into the desert floor, depicting animals, geometric shapes, and mysterious symbols.

From the vantage point of a small plane, travelers can marvel at the sheer scale and precision of these ancient artworks, which date back to the Nazca culture of pre-Columbian Peru. While the purpose and meaning of the Nazca Lines remain a mystery, their sheer beauty and intricacy continue to captivate and inspire visitors from around the world.

Aerial tours of the Nazca Lines offer a unique perspective on Peru's rich cultural heritage and ancient civilizations, providing travelers with a once-in-a-lifetime opportunity to witness one of the world's most intriguing archaeological mysteries from above.

D. Rock Climbing and Caving

Peru's rugged landscapes and diverse geology offer exciting opportunities for rock climbing and caving enthusiasts. From towering granite walls to labyrinthine underground caverns, Peru's outdoor adventures promise adrenaline-pumping challenges and breathtaking discoveries for adventurers of all levels.

Rock Climbing in Huaraz:

Huaraz, nestled in the heart of the Peruvian Andes, is a mecca for rock climbers seeking thrilling ascents amidst stunning alpine scenery. The region boasts an abundance of granite cliffs, soaring peaks, and craggy outcrops that offer a variety of climbing experiences, from beginner-friendly routes to challenging multi-pitch ascents.

One of the most iconic climbing destinations in Huaraz is the Cordillera Blanca, home to towering peaks such as Alpamayo, Huascarán, and Huandoy. The granite walls of the Cordillera

Blanca provide world-class climbing opportunities, with routes ranging from traditional crack climbs to bolted sport routes.

For those seeking a more immersive experience, multi-day climbing expeditions in the Cordillera Blanca offer the chance to summit some of the highest peaks in South America while honing technical climbing skills and acclimatizing to high altitude.

Caving in the Amazon Rainforest:

Beneath the dense canopy of the Amazon rainforest lie hidden worlds of limestone caverns and underground rivers, waiting to be explored by adventurous cavers. Peru's Amazon region is home to an extensive network of caves, some of which remain uncharted and undiscovered.

Exploring the caves of the Amazon rainforest offers a unique opportunity to witness the subterranean wonders of one of the world's most biodiverse ecosystems. From cathedral-like chambers adorned with stalactites and stalagmites to winding passages shrouded in darkness, each cave holds its own secrets and surprises for intrepid explorers.

Guided caving expeditions provide the opportunity to delve deep into the heart of the Amazon, where adventurers can marvel at the intricate formations carved by centuries of geological processes and encounter unique species adapted to life underground.

Adventure Tourism in Oxapampa:

Oxapampa, located in the central highlands of Peru, is emerging as a premier destination for adventure tourism, offering a wide range of outdoor activities including rock climbing, caving, and zip-lining.

The region's diverse landscapes, which include lush cloud forests, rugged mountains, and pristine rivers, provide the perfect backdrop for adrenaline-fueled adventures. Rock climbers can test their skills on the granite cliffs of Cerro

Colorado, while cavers can explore the labyrinthine caves of Pozuzo Valley.

For those seeking a bird's-eye view of the stunning scenery, zip-lining tours offer an exhilarating way to soar through the treetops and experience the beauty of Oxapampa from above.

In Oxapampa, adventure awaits around every corner, beckoning travelers to explore its natural wonders and embark on unforgettable outdoor escapades amidst some of Peru's most breathtaking landscapes.

Peru's diverse outdoor adventures offer something for everyone, from adrenaline-pumping rock climbs to tranquil explorations of underground caverns. Whether you're scaling granite cliffs in the Andes or delving into the depths of the Amazon rainforest, Peru promises unforgettable experiences for adventurers seeking thrills, challenges, and discoveries off the beaten path.

In Peru, adventure awaits at every turn, beckoning travelers to explore its natural wonders and embark on unforgettable outdoor escapades.

This chapter aims to guide adventurers through the diverse array of outdoor activities available in Peru, providing essential information and insights to help you make the most of your thrilling journey through this enchanting country.

Chapter 12: Understanding Peruvian Culture

Peru's rich cultural heritage is a tapestry woven from the threads of its indigenous traditions, colonial history, and modern influences. Understanding Peruvian culture is key to immersing oneself in the vibrant and diverse tapestry of this South American nation.

A. Festivals and Celebrations

Peru's festivals and celebrations are a vibrant tapestry woven from the threads of its diverse cultural heritage. From the soaring peaks of the Andes to the sun-kissed shores of the Pacific coast, every region of Peru boasts its own unique traditions and festivities, offering travelers an immersive glimpse into the country's rich tapestry of culture and history.

Inti Raymi

At the heart of Peruvian culture lies Inti Raymi, the Festival of the Sun. Celebrated annually on June 24th, Inti Raymi was one of the most important ceremonies in the Inca Empire, dedicated to honoring Inti, the Sun God. Today, the festival is reenacted with grandeur in the ancient Incan capital of Cusco, drawing thousands of visitors from around the world.

The celebration begins with a colorful procession from the historic Plaza de Armas to the sacred site of Sacsayhuamán, where the main ceremony takes place. Dressed in elaborate traditional costumes, participants pay homage to the Sun God through music, dance, and ritualistic offerings. The air is filled with the sounds of panpipes and drums, as performers reenact ancient Incan rituals, invoking blessings for the coming year.

Carnival

Carnival is a joyous celebration that sweeps across Peru in the weeks leading up to Lent. Known for its exuberant street parties, water fights, and elaborate costumes, Carnival is a time of revelry and merrymaking. In cities and towns throughout the country, colorful parades wind through the streets, accompanied by the infectious rhythms of Afro-Peruvian music and Andean folk tunes.

One of the most iconic Carnival celebrations can be found in the coastal city of Cajamarca, where the festivities are marked by the playful tradition of water battles. Revelers armed with buckets, balloons, and water guns take to the streets, engaging in spirited water fights that symbolize the cleansing and renewal of the spirit.

Virgen de la Candelaria

In the highland city of Puno, nestled along the shores of Lake Titicaca, the Virgen de la Candelaria festival takes center stage each February. As one of the largest and most colorful festivals in Peru, Virgen de la Candelaria attracts thousands of pilgrims and spectators from across the Andean region.

The festival's highlights include dazzling parades featuring intricately costumed dancers known as 'diabladas' and 'morenadas,' who pay homage to the Virgin Mary through elaborate choreography and vibrant displays of color. Traditional music fills the air, as brass bands and percussion ensembles accompany the procession, creating an electrifying atmosphere of joy and devotion.

Peru's festivals and celebrations serve as a vibrant expression of its cultural heritage and collective identity. Whether honoring ancient deities, celebrating the changing seasons, or commemorating religious traditions, these events offer a window into the heart and soul of the Peruvian people. From the majestic mountains of the Andes to the bustling streets of its cities, Peru's festivals are a testament to the country's enduring spirit of resilience, creativity, and community.

B. Music and Dance

Peruvian music and dance are integral components of the country's cultural identity, reflecting a rich tapestry of indigenous, European, and African influences. From the soaring melodies of the Andean highlands to the rhythmic beats of the coastal plains, Peru's musical landscape is as diverse and dynamic as its geography.

Huayno

Originating in the Andean regions of Peru, Huayno is a traditional folk music genre that resonates with the spirit of the highlands. Characterized by its plaintive melodies, intricate rhythms, and evocative lyrics, Huayno captures the essence of Andean life and folklore. The music is often accompanied by indigenous instruments such as the charango, quena, and zampona, creating a soul-stirring soundtrack that celebrates the natural beauty and cultural richness of the Andes.

Huayno is not only a form of music but also a dance that holds deep significance in Andean communities. The dance is marked by graceful footwork, intricate patterns, and vibrant costumes adorned with intricate embroidery and bright colors. With each step and sway, dancers pay homage to their ancestral roots and the timeless rhythms of the mountains.

Marinera

In contrast to the highlands, the coastal regions of Peru are home to the graceful and romantic dance known as Marinera. Influenced by Spanish colonial traditions, Marinera is characterized by its elegant movements, intricate choreography, and flirtatious exchanges between partners. Dancers move with grace and precision, evoking the spirit of courtship and romance that lies at the heart of the dance.

Accompanied by the melodic strains of guitars, violins, and cajón percussion, Marinera transports audiences to the sun-drenched beaches and bustling plazas of coastal Peru. The dance is often performed during festivals and celebrations, where couples compete in lively competitions known as Marinera Contests, showcasing their skill, style, and passion for this beloved cultural tradition.

Afro-Peruvian Music

Embedded within Peru's cultural tapestry is the rich musical tradition of Afro-Peruvian music, which traces its roots to the descendants of African slaves brought to the country during the colonial era. Characterized by its soulful rhythms, syncopated beats, and haunting melodies, Afro-Peruvian music is a powerful expression of resilience, creativity, and cultural pride.

One of the most iconic Afro-Peruvian musical genres is the landó, a slow and sensual dance accompanied by the rhythmic tapping of wooden boxes known as cajónes. With its origins in the coastal regions of Peru, the landó reflects the experiences and emotions of Afro-Peruvian communities, celebrating their heritage and contributions to the country's cultural mosaic.

In addition to the landó, Afro-Peruvian music encompasses a diverse array of styles and influences, including the festejo, the zamacueca, and the vals criollo. From the bustling streets of Lima to the remote villages of the Peruvian coast, Afro-Peruvian music continues to inspire and captivate audiences, serving as a powerful reminder of Peru's multicultural heritage and enduring spirit.

C. Arts and Crafts

Peru's arts and crafts are a testament to the country's rich cultural heritage and artisanal traditions. From the intricate textiles of the Andean highlands to the exquisite pottery of the coastal plains, Peruvian craftsmanship reflects centuries of creativity, ingenuity, and cultural exchange.

Textiles

Peruvian textiles are renowned for their vibrant colors, intricate patterns, and meticulous craftsmanship. Rooted in ancient Andean traditions, textile weaving has been practiced for thousands of years, passed down through generations as a sacred art form and a means of cultural expression.

In communities like Chinchero and Ollantaytambo, skilled weavers use traditional backstrap looms to create textiles that tell stories of Andean life, mythology, and folklore. Each thread is carefully dyed using natural pigments derived from plants, insects, and minerals, resulting in a dazzling array of colors and textures that reflect the diverse landscapes of the Andes.

From the iconic ponchos and mantas of the highlands to the intricately woven tapestries and blankets of the Sacred Valley, Peruvian textiles are prized for their beauty, quality, and cultural significance. Today, artisans continue to preserve and innovate upon these ancient techniques, blending traditional designs with contemporary styles to create timeless works of art.

Pottery

Peruvian pottery is a testament to the country's rich archaeological heritage and cultural diversity. Dating back thousands of years, Peruvian ceramics encompass a wide range of styles, techniques, and traditions, reflecting the ingenuity and creativity of ancient civilizations such as the Moche, Chimu, and Nazca.

In the coastal desert regions of Peru, artisans craft pottery using techniques passed down through generations, shaping and firing clay into vessels, figurines, and ceremonial objects that reflect the natural world and spiritual beliefs of their ancestors. From the intricate geometric designs of the Nazca to the lifelike portrayals of animals and humans by the Moche, Peruvian pottery is a window into the artistic achievements of pre-Columbian civilizations.

Today, Peruvian pottery continues to thrive as a vibrant and evolving art form, with artisans blending traditional techniques with contemporary aesthetics to create innovative and inspired works of art. Whether exploring the bustling markets of Lima or the remote villages of the Sacred Valley, visitors to Peru can discover a treasure trove of pottery that speaks to the country's rich cultural heritage and artistic legacy.

D. Wood Carving

In the lush forests of the Amazon and the rugged landscapes of the Andes, wood carving has been a cherished tradition for centuries, providing artisans with a medium to express their creativity and reverence for the natural world.

In communities like Ayacucho and Chulucanas, skilled carvers transform native woods such as cedar, mahogany, and alder into intricate sculptures, masks, and religious icons that reflect the spiritual beliefs and cultural traditions of their communities. Using simple hand tools and techniques passed down through generations, these artisans imbue each piece with a sense of craftsmanship and authenticity that speaks to Peru's rich cultural heritage.

From the whimsical figures of animals and birds to the solemn visages of saints and deities, Peruvian wood carving encompasses a diverse range of styles and subjects, each infused with the unique identity and worldview of its creator. Today, wood carving remains a vital and cherished art form in Peru, serving as a powerful reminder of the country's deep connection to the natural world and its enduring spirit of creativity and craftsmanship.

Exploring Peru's festivals, music, dance, and arts and crafts offers travelers a deeper appreciation of its cultural richness and diversity. Whether wandering through bustling markets or witnessing ancient rituals, experiencing Peruvian culture is a journey of discovery and delight.

Chapter 13: Practical Tips for Traveling in Peru

Traveling in Peru offers a rich tapestry of experiences, from exploring ancient ruins to discovering vibrant cultures and breathtaking landscapes. To make the most of your journey, it's essential to be well-prepared and informed about health and safety precautions, packing essentials, as well as local etiquette and customs.

A. Health and Safety

Ensuring your health and safety is paramount while traveling in Peru. With its diverse geography, high altitudes, and unique environmental conditions, being prepared can make all the difference in enjoying your journey without any setbacks.

Altitude Sickness

One of the most common health concerns for travelers to Peru is altitude sickness, also known as acute mountain sickness (AMS). Many of Peru's popular destinations, including Cusco, Machu Picchu, and Lake Titicaca, are situated at high altitudes. Symptoms of altitude sickness can include headaches, nausea, fatigue, and dizziness.

To minimize the risk of altitude sickness:

- Acclimatize gradually: If possible, spend a day or two in a lower altitude city like Lima before ascending to higher elevations. This allows your body to adjust to the thinner air.

- Stay hydrated: Drink plenty of water to help combat dehydration, a common exacerbating factor of altitude sickness.

- Avoid alcohol and heavy meals: Alcohol and heavy meals can impair your body's ability to acclimatize to high altitudes. Opt for light, easily digestible meals instead.

- Consider medication: Some travelers may benefit from medications like acetazolamide (Diamox) to prevent or alleviate symptoms of altitude sickness. Consult with a healthcare professional before taking any medications.

Food and Water Safety

While Peruvian cuisine is renowned for its flavors and variety, travelers should exercise caution when consuming food and water to avoid gastrointestinal issues. Here are some tips for staying safe:

- Drink bottled or purified water: Stick to bottled water or water that has been boiled, filtered, or treated with purification tablets.

- Eat at reputable establishments: Choose restaurants and food vendors that appear clean and well-maintained. Avoid raw or undercooked foods, and opt for freshly prepared dishes.

- Wash fruits and vegetables: If consuming raw fruits and vegetables, wash them thoroughly with bottled or purified water to remove any contaminants.

Sun Protection

Peru's proximity to the equator means strong sun exposure, especially at higher elevations. Sunburn and UV radiation can pose significant health risks if proper precautions are not taken. To protect yourself from sun damage:

- Use sunscreen: Apply a broad-spectrum sunscreen with a high SPF (Sun Protection Factor) to exposed skin, including your face, neck, and hands. Reapply sunscreen every few hours, especially after swimming or sweating.

- Wear protective clothing: Cover up with lightweight, long-sleeved shirts, pants, and wide-brimmed hats to shield your skin from the sun's harmful rays.

- Use sunglasses: Invest in a pair of sunglasses that block 100% of UVA and UVB rays to protect your eyes from sun damage and reduce the risk of cataracts and other eye conditions.

- Seek shade: Limit exposure to direct sunlight during peak hours (usually between 10 a.m. and 4 p.m.) by seeking shade under trees, umbrellas, or awnings.

Medical Precautions

It's essential to be prepared for medical emergencies and minor health issues while traveling in Peru. Consider the following precautions:

- Carry a medical kit: Pack a basic medical kit containing essentials like pain relievers, anti-diarrheal medication, antihistamines, adhesive bandages, and any prescription medications you may need.

- Purchase travel insurance: Invest in comprehensive travel insurance that covers medical emergencies, hospitalization, and medical evacuation to ensure you receive prompt and appropriate medical care if needed.

By prioritizing your health and safety and taking necessary precautions, you can enjoy your travels in Peru with peace of mind and make the most of your adventure in this captivating destination.

B. Packing Essentials

Packing efficiently and thoughtfully can greatly enhance your travel experience in Peru. Whether you're exploring ancient ruins, trekking through the Andes, or navigating bustling city streets, having the right gear can make your journey more comfortable and enjoyable. Here are some essential items to consider packing for your trip to Peru:

Layered Clothing

Peru's diverse geography and varying altitudes mean that temperatures can fluctuate significantly from one region to another and even throughout the day. Packing layers allows you to adapt to changing weather conditions and stay comfortable in any situation. Consider including the following clothing items in your luggage:

- Lightweight shirts and tops: Breathable, moisture-wicking fabrics are ideal for staying cool and comfortable, especially in warmer climates like the Amazon rainforest and coastal regions.

- Long-sleeved shirts and sweaters: These are essential for layering and providing warmth during cooler evenings or at higher elevations in the Andes.

- Waterproof jacket or rain poncho: Be prepared for sudden rain showers, especially if you're visiting during the wet season (November to April) or exploring rainforest regions like the Amazon.

- Convertible pants: Opt for pants that can be converted into shorts for versatility and comfort in different climates and activities.

Sturdy Footwear

Choosing the right footwear is crucial for exploring Peru's diverse terrain, which includes rugged mountains, ancient ruins, and cobblestone streets. Invest in sturdy, supportive footwear that can handle a variety of conditions:

- Hiking boots: If you plan to trek in the Andes or explore remote wilderness areas, durable hiking boots with ankle support are essential for comfort and stability on uneven terrain.

- Comfortable walking shoes: For urban exploration and sightseeing in cities like Lima and Cusco, lightweight and comfortable walking shoes are a must. Choose shoes with good arch support and cushioning for long days of sightseeing.

- Waterproof sandals or water shoes: Ideal for activities like visiting hot springs, navigating muddy trails, or exploring coastal areas where you may encounter water.

Travel Adapters and Chargers

Don't forget to pack the necessary adapters and chargers to keep your electronic devices powered up throughout your journey in Peru. The country uses Type A and Type C electrical outlets, so ensure you have the appropriate adapters for your devices. Consider packing the following items:

- Universal travel adapter: A versatile adapter that can accommodate various plug types will ensure you can charge your devices wherever you go in Peru.

- Multi-port USB charger: A compact USB charger with multiple ports allows you to charge multiple devices simultaneously, saving space and reducing clutter in your accommodation.

Daypack

A lightweight daypack is indispensable for carrying essential items and personal belongings during day trips, excursions, and sightseeing adventures. Look for a pack that is comfortable to wear and offers enough storage space for the following items:

- Water bottle: Stay hydrated throughout the day by carrying a reusable water bottle filled with purified water.

- Snacks: Pack energy-boosting snacks like trail mix, granola bars, and fresh fruit to keep you fueled during long days of exploration.

- Sun protection: Don't forget to pack sunscreen, sunglasses, a wide-brimmed hat, and a lightweight scarf or shawl for added protection from the sun.

By packing smart and considering the specific activities and destinations on your itinerary, you can ensure that you have everything you need for a comfortable, convenient, and memorable adventure in Peru.

C. Etiquette and Customs

Understanding and respecting local customs and etiquette is key to enjoying meaningful interactions and fostering goodwill during your travels in Peru. With its rich cultural heritage and diverse population, Peru has its own unique customs and social norms. Here are some important etiquette guidelines to keep in mind:

Greetings and Politeness

Peruvians place great importance on greetings and politeness in social interactions. When meeting someone for the first time or entering a room, it is customary to greet others with a handshake and a friendly "buenos días" (good morning), "buenas tardes" (good afternoon), or "buenas noches" (good evening), depending on the time of day. Use titles such as "Senor" (Mr.), "Senora" (Mrs.), or

"Senorita" (Miss) followed by the person's last name unless invited to use their first name.

Respect for Sacred Sites

Peru is home to numerous archaeological sites and sacred places that hold deep cultural and spiritual significance for its people. When visiting sites such as Machu Picchu, Sacsayhuaman, or the Nazca Lines, it is important to show respect and reverence:

- Follow posted rules and regulations, including prohibitions on touching or climbing on structures, to help preserve these ancient treasures for future generations.

- Dispose of trash responsibly and leave the site as you found it, respecting the natural and cultural environment.

- Engage with local guides and respect their knowledge and expertise about the history and significance of the site.

Tipping and Gratuities

Tipping is customary in Peru, especially in restaurants, hotels, and for services like guided tours and transportation. While tipping practices may vary depending on the region and the level of service received, a gratuity of 10-15% of the total bill is generally appreciated for good service. When tipping, consider the following:

- In restaurants, check if a service charge has already been included in the bill. If not, leaving a cash tip directly for the server is customary.

- Tip porters, drivers, and tour guides for their assistance and services, especially if they have provided exceptional service or gone above and beyond to ensure your comfort and satisfaction.

Language and Communication

While Spanish is the official language of Peru, indigenous languages such as Quechua and

Aymara are also spoken in certain regions, particularly in the Andean highlands. Learning a few basic phrases in Spanish, such as greetings and polite expressions, can help you connect with locals and demonstrate respect for their culture and language. Here are some helpful phrases to know:

- "Hola" - Hello
- "Por favor" - Please
- "Gracias" - Thank you
- "Disculpe" - Excuse me/pardon me
- "¿Cuánto cuesta?" - How much does it cost?

By embracing local customs and showing respect for Peruvian culture, you can create meaningful connections with the people you meet and enrich your travel experience in this vibrant and diverse country.

D. Currency and Money Matters

Navigating currency and managing your finances effectively is essential for a smooth and enjoyable travel experience in Peru. Here are some important considerations and tips to help you handle money matters during your visit:

Currency

The official currency of Peru is the Peruvian Sol (PEN), which is abbreviated as S/. Banknotes and coins are used for transactions, with banknotes available in denominations of 10, 20, 50, 100, and 200 Soles, and coins in denominations of 1, 2, and 5 Soles, as well as smaller centavo coins.

Exchange Rates

Before traveling to Peru, familiarize yourself with the current exchange rates to understand the value of the Peruvian Sol relative to your home currency. Exchange rates can fluctuate, so it's advisable to check rates from reputable sources such as banks or currency exchange offices for the most accurate information.

Where to Exchange Currency

Currency exchange services are widely available in Peru, including at airports, banks, hotels, exchange offices (casas de cambio), and some larger stores and supermarkets. While exchange rates may vary slightly between providers, banks and exchange offices generally offer competitive rates and lower fees compared to airports and hotels.

ATMs and Cash Withdrawals

ATMs (cajeros automáticos) are prevalent in major cities and tourist destinations throughout Peru and are a convenient way to access cash. Look for ATMs affiliated with major networks such as Visa, MasterCard, or Cirrus, which are widely accepted. Keep the following tips in mind when using ATMs:

- Check with your bank before traveling to ensure your debit or credit card will work in Peru and to inquire about any fees or foreign transaction charges.

- Use ATMs located inside banks or reputable establishments for security and peace of mind.

- Be vigilant and aware of your surroundings when withdrawing cash, especially in busy or tourist areas, to avoid potential theft or scams.

Credit Cards and Payment Options

Credit cards, especially Visa and MasterCard, are widely accepted in hotels, restaurants, shops, and larger establishments in urban areas and tourist destinations. However, it's always advisable to carry some cash for smaller purchases, street vendors, or establishments that may not accept cards. Notify your bank of your travel plans to avoid any issues with card authorization and security measures.

Safety and Security

When handling money and conducting financial transactions in Peru, prioritize safety and security to protect yourself from theft, fraud, or other risks:

- Keep your cash, cards, and valuables secure at all times, preferably in a money belt, hidden pouch, or secure pocket.

- Avoid displaying large amounts of cash in public and be discreet when handling money, especially in crowded or touristy areas.

- Be cautious when sharing personal or financial information, especially in unfamiliar or unsecured environments, and only use reputable and secure ATMs and payment terminals.

By familiarizing yourself with currency exchange procedures, payment options, and safety precautions, you can confidently manage your finances and enjoy a worry-free travel experience in Peru.

In conclusion, by embracing these practical tips and cultural insights, you can embark on a memorable journey through Peru while staying safe, comfortable, and respectful of local customs.

Chapter 14: Itineraries for Peru

Peru offers a rich tapestry of experiences, from its ancient archaeological wonders to its vibrant cultural traditions and stunning natural landscapes. Whether you have a week or several weeks to explore, Peru has itineraries tailored to suit every traveler's preferences and interests.

A. 7-Day Highlights Tour

Embarking on a 7-day highlights tour of Peru promises a whirlwind adventure packed with historical marvels, cultural discoveries, and natural wonders. This condensed itinerary is perfect for travelers with limited time who want to experience the essence of Peru's most iconic destinations.

Day 1: Lima Arrival

Your journey begins in Lima, the sprawling metropolis that serves as Peru's vibrant capital.

Upon arrival, you'll be greeted by the city's bustling energy, a fusion of colonial grandeur and modern dynamism. Lima's eclectic neighborhoods beckon exploration, from the historic streets of the city center to the trendy districts of Miraflores and Barranco.

Day 2: Lima City Tour

Dive into Lima's rich history with a guided city tour. Explore the Plaza Mayor, the heart of colonial Lima, flanked by architectural gems such as the Government Palace and the Cathedral of Lima. Delve into the city's past at the San Francisco Monastery, where underground catacombs reveal centuries of history and intrigue.

Day 3: Cusco

Bid farewell to Lima as you board a flight to Cusco, the ancient capital of the Inca Empire. Nestled high in the Andes, Cusco captivates with its cobblestone streets, Inca ruins, and Spanish colonial architecture. Take time to acclimate to the altitude as you wander through the city's lively plazas and vibrant markets, soaking in the Andean culture that permeates every corner.

Day 4: Sacred Valley

Embark on a scenic journey through the Sacred Valley, a verdant expanse dotted with picturesque villages and Inca ruins. Explore the terraced hillsides of Pisac, where an artisanal market bursts with color and tradition. Continue to Ollantaytambo, a living testament to Inca engineering prowess, where massive stone walls guard the entrance to a storied past.

Day 5: Machu Picchu

Rise early for a once-in-a-lifetime adventure to Machu Picchu, the crown jewel of Inca civilization. Board a train from Ollantaytambo to Aguas Calientes, the gateway to this ancient citadel nestled amidst mist-shrouded mountains. As you ascend to the citadel, be prepared to be awe-struck by Machu Picchu's enigmatic beauty and mystical ambiance. Explore its labyrinthine streets, marvel at its architectural wonders, and contemplate the mysteries of its lost civilization.

Day 6: Return to Lima

Bid farewell to the wonders of Machu Picchu as you journey back to Lima, your heart full of memories and your camera brimming with snapshots of Peru's unparalleled beauty. Spend your final day in Lima indulging in its culinary delights, from traditional ceviche to innovative gastronomic creations that showcase Peru's diverse culinary heritage.

Day 7: Departure

As your 7-day highlights tour draws to a close, reflect on the myriad experiences that have shaped your journey through Peru. From the ancient wonders of Machu Picchu to the colonial charm of Lima, each moment has been a testament to the richness and diversity of this enchanting country. Depart from Lima with a sense of gratitude and wonder, knowing that Peru's timeless allure will linger in your heart long after you've said goodbye.

B. 14-Day Cultural Immersion

Embark on a 14-day cultural immersion journey through Peru, where ancient traditions, colonial heritage, and natural wonders converge to create an unforgettable tapestry of experiences. This extended itinerary allows for a deeper exploration of Peru's diverse landscapes and rich cultural heritage, offering travelers the opportunity to delve beneath the surface and connect with the soul of the country.

Days 1-7: Same as the 7-Day Highlights Tour

Follow the itinerary of the 7-Day Highlights Tour, allowing for a more leisurely exploration of Lima, Cusco, and the Sacred Valley. Take time to savor the nuances of each destination, from Lima's culinary delights to Cusco's Andean charm, immersing yourself in the rhythms of daily life and the warmth of Peruvian hospitality.

Day 8: Lake Titicaca

Venture to the shores of Lake Titicaca, the highest navigable lake in the world and a sacred symbol of Andean spirituality. Explore the floating Uros Islands, where indigenous communities have lived for centuries atop totora reed rafts, and marvel at the traditional way of life that continues to thrive amidst the tranquil waters of the lake. Continue to Taquile Island, where time seems to stand still amid terraced hillsides and ancient Inca terraces, and immerse yourself in the vibrant culture of the local Quechua-speaking communities.

Days 9-10: Arequipa

Journey to Arequipa, known as the "White City" for its dazzling colonial architecture crafted from volcanic sillar stone. Explore the historic center, a UNESCO World Heritage Site, where baroque churches and elegant mansions line cobblestone streets. Visit the Santa Catalina Monastery, a city within a city, where cloistered nuns once lived in seclusion amidst colorful courtyards and ornate chapels, offering a glimpse into a bygone era.

Days 11-14: Amazon Rainforest

Fly to Puerto Maldonado and embark on a once-in-a-lifetime adventure into the heart of the Amazon Rainforest. Traverse winding rivers and dense jungle trails, encountering an astonishing array of flora and fauna along the way. Explore pristine oxbow lakes teeming with wildlife, spot playful river otters frolicking in the water, and listen to the symphony of jungle sounds as night falls. Learn from indigenous guides about the delicate balance of this biodiverse ecosystem and gain insight into age-old traditions passed down through generations.

Overall, as your 14-day cultural immersion journey comes to a close, reflect on the depth and diversity of experiences that have shaped your understanding of Peru's rich cultural tapestry. From the Andean highlands to the depths of the Amazon, each encounter has been a revelation, illuminating the interconnectedness of Peru's natural and cultural heritage. Depart from Peru with a newfound appreciation for the country's boundless beauty and the enduring spirit of its people, knowing that the memories of your journey will linger long after you've returned home.

C. 21-Day Adventure Expedition

Prepare for the ultimate 21-day adventure expedition through Peru, where rugged landscapes, ancient civilizations, and adrenaline-pumping activities await at every turn. This extended itinerary is tailor-made for thrill-seekers and outdoor enthusiasts eager to explore Peru's diverse terrain and push the boundaries of adventure.

Days 1-14: Same as the 14-Day Cultural Immersion

Embark on the first 14 days following the Cultural Immersion itinerary, delving deep into Peru's cultural and natural wonders. From the heights of the Andes to the depths of the Amazon, immerse yourself in the heart and soul of this captivating country, savoring each moment of discovery along the way.

Day 15: Nazca Lines

Embark on an aerial adventure over the enigmatic Nazca Lines, ancient geoglyphs etched into the desert plains of southern Peru. From the vantage point of a small aircraft, marvel at the intricate designs and colossal figures that stretch across the landscape below, pondering the mysteries of their creation and significance to the ancient Nazca civilization.

Days 16-18: Colca Canyon

Journey to Colca Canyon, one of the world's deepest canyons, where soaring condors ride thermal currents against a backdrop of rugged cliffs and terraced fields. Embark on exhilarating treks along the canyon rim, descending into its depths to discover remote villages and natural hot springs hidden amid the rugged terrain. As the sun sets over the canyon, witness the majestic flight of the condors, a timeless spectacle that symbolizes the enduring spirit of the Andean highlands.

Days 19-21: Huascarán National Park

Travel to Huaraz and explore the dramatic landscapes of Huascarán National Park, home to Peru's highest peaks and most stunning alpine scenery. Lace up your hiking boots and embark on epic treks amidst towering glaciers, turquoise lakes, and rugged mountain passes. Marvel at the beauty of Laguna 69, nestled beneath the towering peaks of the Cordillera Blanca, and feel the rush of adrenaline as you conquer high-altitude mountain passes and navigate pristine wilderness trails.

As your 21-day adventure expedition draws to a close, reflect on the myriad challenges and triumphs that have defined your journey through Peru's wild and untamed landscapes. From the ancient mysteries of the Nazca Lines to the rugged beauty of Colca Canyon and Huascarán National

Park, each day has been an exploration of the extraordinary. Depart from Peru with a sense of awe and accomplishment, knowing that the memories of your epic adventure will stay with you for a lifetime, inspiring future journeys and igniting a passion for exploration that knows no bounds.

In conclusion, embark on an unforgettable journey through Peru's diverse landscapes, rich history, and vibrant culture with these curated itineraries. Each offers a unique perspective and a deeper understanding of this captivating country.

Chapter 15: Farewell and Resources

Congratulations! You've embarked on an incredible journey through the enchanting landscapes, vibrant cultures, and rich history of Peru. As your adventure draws to a close, this chapter provides essential resources, further reading suggestions, and acknowledgments to enhance your travel experiences and express gratitude to those who have contributed to your exploration of Peru.

A. Travel Resources

Peru, with its diverse landscapes, rich history, and vibrant culture, beckons travelers from around the globe to embark on unforgettable adventures. Navigating the intricacies of Peruvian travel requires access to reliable resources that can enhance your journey, ensuring smooth logistics, memorable experiences, and meaningful interactions with the country's wonders.

Peru Tourism Board (PromPeru)

At the forefront of promoting Peru's tourism industry stands the Peru Tourism Board, known as PromPeru. This official government agency serves as a comprehensive source of information for travelers seeking to explore the myriad attractions and destinations scattered across Peru's varied terrain.

PromPeru's website serves as a gateway to a wealth of resources, including destination guides, travel advisories, cultural events calendars, and practical tips for travelers. Whether you're planning a trek through the Andes, a culinary exploration in Lima, or a cultural immersion in the Amazon rainforest, PromPeru offers valuable insights to help you navigate Peru's diverse landscapes and vibrant cultural tapestry.

Local Tourism Offices

As you venture beyond the beaten path and delve into the heart of Peru's regions and provinces, local tourism offices emerge as invaluable allies in your travel endeavors. These offices, scattered throughout the country, serve as hubs of information, connecting travelers with local insights, recommendations, and assistance tailored to each unique destination.

From the bustling streets of Cusco to the remote villages of the Sacred Valley, local tourism offices provide invaluable guidance on accommodations, transportation options, dining experiences, and off-the-beaten-path attractions. Whether you're seeking to explore ancient archaeological sites, embark on adrenaline-pumping outdoor adventures, or immerse yourself in indigenous cultures, the friendly staff at these offices are eager to help you craft unforgettable experiences that resonate with the soul of Peru.

Travel Agencies and Tour Operators

For travelers seeking curated experiences, personalized itineraries, and expert guidance, Peru's array of travel agencies and tour operators offer a gateway to seamless exploration and immersive cultural encounters. These professionals possess intimate knowledge of Peru's hidden gems, cultural nuances, and logistical intricacies, ensuring that every aspect of your journey is meticulously planned and executed with precision.

Whether you're embarking on a luxury train journey to Machu Picchu, navigating the enigmatic Nazca Lines from the sky, or embarking on a gastronomic odyssey through Lima's culinary scene, travel agencies and tour operators can tailor experiences to match your interests, preferences, and travel style. From knowledgeable guides to comfortable accommodations and seamless transportation, these professionals elevate your Peruvian adventure to new heights of discovery and delight.

Online Travel Communities

In the digital age, the world of travel has been transformed by online communities and forums dedicated to sharing insights, exchanging tips, and fostering connections among like-minded adventurers. Peru's vibrant online travel community serves as a virtual gathering place for travelers to seek advice, share experiences, and forge friendships that transcend borders and boundaries.

Whether you're seeking recommendations for hidden gems in the Sacred Valley, tips for acclimating to high-altitude environments, or insights into Peruvian cuisine and culture, online travel communities provide a wealth of knowledge and camaraderie. From social media groups to specialized forums and travel blogs, the virtual landscape of Peru beckons travelers to embark on a journey of discovery and connection that transcends the confines of time and space.

Mobile Apps

In an age of smartphones and digital connectivity, mobile apps have become indispensable tools for travelers navigating the labyrinthine landscapes of Peru. From language translation and currency conversion to real-time navigation and travel updates, mobile apps empower travelers with the information and resources needed to navigate Peru with confidence and ease.

Whether you're exploring the cobblestone streets of Cusco, navigating the bustling markets of Arequipa, or embarking on a jungle expedition in the Amazon basin, mobile apps offer a wealth of features to enhance your travel experience. From offline maps and GPS navigation to language-learning tools and cultural insights, these digital companions ensure that every step of your Peruvian journey is informed, connected, and enriched by the wonders of modern technology.

In the vast tapestry of Peruvian travel, these resources serve as beacons of guidance, inspiration, and connectivity, inviting travelers to embark on a journey of discovery, enlightenment, and transformation. As you chart your course through the enchanting landscapes and storied history of

Peru, may these resources illuminate your path and enrich your adventures with the splendor and spirit of this captivating country.

B. Further Reading

Peru's allure extends far beyond its breathtaking landscapes and ancient ruins, captivating travelers with its rich tapestry of history, culture, and intrigue. For those eager to delve deeper into the heart and soul of Peru, a wealth of literature awaits, offering insights, revelations, and perspectives that illuminate the country's myriad wonders.

"Turn Right at Machu Picchu" by Mark Adams

Mark Adams embarks on a riveting journey through the rugged terrain of Peru, tracing the footsteps of Hiram Bingham's legendary expedition to the iconic citadel of Machu Picchu. In "Turn Right at Machu Picchu," Adams weaves together history, adventure, and personal discovery, uncovering the mysteries of one of the world's most enigmatic archaeological wonders.

As Adams navigates the rugged Andean landscape, encounters with local guides, and encounters with the remnants of Inca civilization, readers are treated to a thrilling adventure that transcends time and space. "Turn Right at Machu Picchu" is a testament to the enduring allure of exploration and the transformative power of ancient wonders that continue to captivate the human imagination.

"The Last Days of the Incas" by Kim MacQuarrie

In "The Last Days of the Incas," Kim MacQuarrie transports readers back to the tumultuous era of Spanish conquest and Inca resistance, chronicling the epic clash of civilizations that shaped the destiny of Peru and its people. Through meticulous research and vivid storytelling, MacQuarrie unveils the dramatic events, larger-than-life characters, and enduring legacies of this pivotal moment in history.

From the rise of the Inca Empire to the fall of Vilcabamba, the last bastion of Inca resistance, "The Last Days of the Incas" offers a gripping narrative that sheds light on the complexities of conquest, colonization, and cultural exchange. MacQuarrie's masterful prose and immersive storytelling invite readers to witness the triumphs and tragedies of a bygone era, illuminating the resilience of indigenous peoples and the enduring spirit of Peru.

"Lost City of the Incas" by Hiram Bingham

Hiram Bingham's discovery of Machu Picchu in 1911 captured the world's imagination, thrusting this ancient citadel into the spotlight of global fascination. In "Lost City of the Incas," Bingham offers a firsthand account of his expedition to the remote peaks of the Andes, where he stumbled upon the ruins of a lost civilization hidden amidst the clouds.

Through Bingham's vivid descriptions, archival photographs, and archaeological insights, readers are transported to the mist-shrouded mountains of Peru, where the mysteries of Machu Picchu await discovery. "Lost City of the Incas" serves as a testament to the power of exploration, the allure of ancient mysteries, and the enduring legacy of one of the world's most iconic archaeological sites.

"The Peru Reader: History, Culture, Politics" edited by Orin Starn

"The Peru Reader" offers a comprehensive exploration of Peru's complex history, rich cultural heritage, and dynamic political landscape through a diverse collection of essays, articles, and literary excerpts. Edited by Orin Starn, this anthology delves into the intricacies of Peruvian society, from pre-Columbian civilizations to contemporary debates over identity, inequality, and social justice.

Through the voices of scholars, activists, poets, and politicians, "The Peru Reader" offers a multifaceted portrait of a nation grappling with its past, confronting its present, and envisioning its future. From indigenous resistance movements to urban revolutions, from colonial legacies to indigenous resurgence, this anthology invites readers to engage with the complexities of Peru's history and culture in all its richness and diversity.

"The Conquest of the Incas" by John Hemming

In "The Conquest of the Incas," John Hemming offers a sweeping narrative that chronicles the Spanish conquest of Peru and the tumultuous clash of civilizations that forever altered the course of history. Drawing on a wealth of primary sources and archival research, Hemming provides a nuanced exploration of the conquest's key figures, pivotal moments, and far-reaching consequences.

From Francisco Pizarro's audacious expedition to the capture of the Inca emperor Atahualpa, from the founding of Lima to the establishment of Spanish colonial rule, "The Conquest of the Incas" offers a compelling account of one of the most consequential chapters in Latin American history. Hemming's masterful storytelling and scholarly rigor shed light on the complexities of conquest, colonization, and cultural encounter, inviting readers to grapple with the enduring legacies of Peru's turbulent past.

As you immerse yourself in these captivating narratives and explore the depths of Peru's history, culture, and intrigue, may you embark on a journey of discovery, enlightenment, and transformation. Whether tracing the footsteps of ancient civilizations or unraveling the mysteries of Machu Picchu, may these books serve as windows into the soul of Peru, illuminating its timeless wonders and enduring legacies for generations to come.

As you conclude your exploration of Peru, may the memories of its breathtaking landscapes, vibrant cultures, and ancient wonders linger in your heart forever. Safe travels, and may your next adventure be just around the corner.

CONCLUSION

As you close the final pages of the Peru Travel Guide 2024, I extend to you a warm embrace and heartfelt congratulations on your journey through the captivating landscapes, rich history, and vibrant cultures of Peru. Your decision to embark on this exploration of one of South America's most enchanting destinations speaks volumes about your adventurous spirit and thirst for discovery.

Throughout the pages of this guide, we have endeavored to be your faithful companion, offering insights, recommendations, and inspiration to fuel your Peruvian odyssey. From the mist-shrouded peaks of the Andes to the lush depths of the Amazon rainforest, from the bustling streets of Lima to the ancient citadel of Machu Picchu, we have endeavored to capture the essence of Peru's diverse tapestry and guide you on a journey of wonder and enlightenment.

In the pages of this book, you have discovered a treasure trove of information, insights, and practical tips to enhance your Peruvian adventure. From detailed itineraries and historical narratives to insider recommendations and cultural insights, we have strived to provide you with the tools and knowledge needed to navigate Peru's myriad wonders with confidence, curiosity, and reverence.

As you traversed the cobblestone streets of Cusco, marveled at the intricate beauty of colonial architecture, and savored the flavors of Peruvian cuisine, we hope that this guide served as your trusted companion, illuminating the hidden gems and cultural nuances that make Peru a truly extraordinary destination.

But beyond the practicalities of travel, we hope that this journey has ignited a deeper connection to the land, the people, and the stories that define Peru's rich tapestry. May the echoes of ancient civilizations resonate within your soul as you stand in awe of Machu Picchu's timeless majesty. May the vibrant colors and rhythms of Peruvian culture infuse your spirit with joy and wonder.

As you bid farewell to Peru, know that the memories forged in its landscapes, the friendships kindled along its trails, and the moments of awe and wonder will linger in your heart forever. May your experiences in Peru serve as a beacon of inspiration, reminding you of the boundless possibilities that await those who dare to explore, discover, and embrace the unknown.

And as you journey onward, may you carry with you the spirit of Peru – resilient, vibrant, and eternally captivating. May each step you take be guided by curiosity, courage, and compassion, illuminating the path ahead with the light of adventure and discovery.

In closing, let us offer a prayer for your continued journey, wherever it may lead:

May the road rise up to meet you,
May the wind be always at your back.

May the sun shine warm upon your face,
And the rains fall soft upon your fields.
And until we meet again,
May you be held in the palm of the Divine's hand.

With heartfelt wishes for safe travels and boundless adventures,

[David C. Anaya]